Feathers
From Heaven

Written by Michael King

Edited by Sunshine L. King

God Signs Series: Book 2

Cover Image: Star Cluster NGC 2074 in the Large Magellanic Cloud

Credit: Nasa, ESA, and M Livio (STScI)

This book and other titles by Michael King can be found at TheKingsofEden.com

Other Titles by Michael King:

Gemstones From Heaven, God Signs Book 1

The Gamer's Guide to the Kingdom of God

Available from Amazon.com, Createspace.com, and other retail outlets.

ISBN-13: 978-1536948349

Printed in the USA

Table of Contents

Dedication

Acknowledgments

Preface

1   Our Personal Story

2   The Meaning in the Manifestation

3   Discernment and Deception

4   Ruffled Feathers

5   Feather Stories

6   How Do I Get This To Happen?

7   Feathers from Heaven

Works Cited

Other Books

Excerpt from Gemstones From Heaven

About the Author

Dedication

I dedicate this book to my grandchildren, Sage, Sophia, and Scarlett. I love you all dearly and greatly enjoy watching you grow up in the Lord. Your laughter, smiles, and silliness are infectious, and you have unique talents and skills that make you wonderfully and uniquely special. God has amazing plans for your life, and I look forward to watching you as you develop.

Acknowledgments

Thank you to the many people who submitted testimonies for this book—I truly believe that your words enrich this work and enhance the fullness that God wants to release in every reader's life.

Thank you to John and Ruth Filler who graciously shared their time, love, and stories of the glorious works of God in their midst, and for the opportunity to photograph the amazing feather God has given you and share the stories with me. May God richly bless you both.

Thank you to Denise Hayes for your amazing graphic design. You always impress me with your artistic eye and skill.

A special thanks to S Loire King. You support me every step of the way, and your editing takes my writing to entirely new levels. I would not be doing this without you.

Preface

Dear Reader,

    As you read, it is my express hope that your life is enriched and your faith is strengthened in God's ability to do far more than you can imagine. My intent in writing this book is to shed light on the feather manifestation and to answer the most common questions people ask about this sign from heaven. My prayer as you read this is that your heart is enriched and this feather sign begins to manifest and increase in your life and that the provision and favor of God floods your home.

Multiple and abundant blessings,

Michael King

Chapter 1

Our Personal Story

"A man with an experience is never at the mercy of an argument."

— Anonymous —

The feathers from heaven began falling for me about ten years ago. The first time I ever saw one appear was in a church I attended while a student in their ministry school. I was at the front of the sanctuary chatting and praying for some people when I saw a tiny wisp of a feather appear in midair at around head height. We all watched as it floated slowly upwards, and then, as if by some trick of the light, the feather became hard to see and then disappeared altogether. I had heard of this phenomenon before but had never seen it. The miracle was pretty astounding.

The second time I found a feather from heaven was after I drove home from visiting a friend, who I am pleased to say is now my wife. She had some pretty intense spiritual activity going on at her house, and feathers, gold dust, and oil were appearing supernaturally with some level of frequency. At any rate, I got in the car and drove home at the end of a night of worship and prayer. As I got out of the car and looked back into the vehicle, a small brown and black feather was on the seat where I had been sitting! I lived in a city at the time and there weren't any birds hanging around that would have conveniently deposited colored feathers inside the car, especially since there was no feather present when I first sat down! I remembered that when I first got in the car I had made a comment about an angel I had just perceived and had looked at the seat before sitting down. Interestingly enough the angel's name was Herald and I suspect he was the one who had left the feather. I kept it in my Bible for years after that.

A number of years later, in 2009, I felt the Lord impress upon me to call a prayer meeting on the day of Pentecost. Only myself, my wife, and a friend showed up, but we all got touched by Holy Spirit. For the next week after I saw a feather float by at some point almost every day—once on the elevator at work, another few times randomly at home, and if I remember correctly, one appeared in my car! All of these were the tiny white wisps, but it was super encouraging to me to see visible fruit for what I had been praying and believing for— namely signs, wonders, and miracles.

Since then I have seen so many feathers I can't even remember half of the times they have appeared. Sometimes it is when we are praying or doing something overtly spiritual;

other times they just appear at random with no sort of special preparation or obvious spiritual precursor. One example of this is a day after my wife and I had been at a Christian conference in the area. We were cuddling on our bed streaming a TV show on our laptop when during the show a feather gently floated across the screen. I lightly pincered it between my thumb and forefinger then opened them to look at it. The feather was gone, but in its place, my fingertips were covered in golden sparkly dust. This dust quickly spread to cover that hand. I looked at the other hand and suddenly it was covered too. My wife held out her hands and they, too, were instantly covered. It finally stopped spreading when both of our arms up to the shoulders were covered in this fine, sparkly, beautiful golden dust. I can't say I understood some deep purpose for that encounter, but it was certainly a nice surprise!

A few years ago I was a nurse case manager at an assisted living facility. I was talking to another nurse, one of my coworkers, about some of the miracles God was doing in our midst, and at that very moment, a feather appeared in midair and floated there. He was pretty astounded. Another nurse entered the office and he immediately started telling her all about it. It was so fun for me to hear him talk because his excitement was genuine. This other nurse wasn't sure about it and asked him if he was trying to fool her. "Oh my God no, I swear on the Holy Bible it's true!" he said with excitement. That comment still makes me smile to this day. There is something about the first time someone experiences a miracle that is so precious and real—the emotions are brutally honest, hard to hide, and the shock and excitement is such a joy to witness. The realness in someone comes to the surface because they aren't hiding behind the masks we so often wear.

When I had just started to work on this book, my wife and I had the blessing of spending all afternoon and evening with a dear friend who was ordained by Ruth Ward Heflin. We spent hours discussing gold dust, gemstones, and hearing her share her own wonderful glory realm stories and memories with Ruth at the Campmeeting in Ashland, Virginia. It was a fantastically glorious time, and my heart was soaring. Late in the evening we prayed for my wife as she had been dealing with some health issues. As we began to break witchcraft off her, I had my eyes closed in prayer. When I opened them and looked down, a feather that was about two inches long had appeared on my arm and caught me totally by surprise. The angels were hard at work warring on her behalf! My wife was ecstatic and said, "They came for me!" She reported that her head felt better after the fact as well.

A few months later, we made some new friends in Coeur D'Alene, Idaho and met the senior pastors of Gateway Christian Fellowship who had their own exciting feather stories that they graciously shared with us, found in Chapter 7. I took some pictures of the feather in their story and was blessed to be able to use it as the cover picture for this book. Yes, the feather on the cover is a real feather from heaven! Not only that, but toward the end of that weekend, we had feathers appear in our hotel room after we had spent much of that time discussing the glory realm and signs, wonders, and miracles.

Feathers continue to appear on an ongoing basis—sometimes more frequent than others, but each time I am reminded of the Father's love for me, the angelic protection that is around me, and that I am surrounded by a realm that is both unseen and highly active in my life. There is something special about this manifestation, both simple and elegant. It has the ability to turn our focus toward God at a moment's notice, interrupting the daily doldrums with the breath of heaven. It is my hope that this book—the divine revelation, our stories, and the stories of others—will open this arena of miracles, angelic visitations, and the glory realm of heaven for every reader, and that they, too, would experience and see an increase in the manifestation of feathers from heaven.

Chapter 2

The Meaning in the Manifestation

I have been finding feathers all over the house, but really only had a down feather throw in my bedroom. I decided to put it away, and tonight I found another feather on the sofa right where I had just been sitting. It reminds me of Psalm 91.

Diana Jamerson

****

Feathers have long been associated with the heaven sent protection of angels. It is no fad or fashion. In the First World War to be given a white feather was supposed to be a token of cowardice and they were frequently presented to conscientious objectors or men who for whatever reason could not be conscripted to the front. But when we view these gifts through the prism of angelic protection, we see that they are in fact a sign of being spared and delivered and retained for some work of the Lord. The angels know what is up.

They are sent ahead of you to meet you where you are at. They seem to have adopted the white feather as an emblem of their presence that can be arranged without fuss or upset. The fact that the feathers call out to people, that they reassure them and invite them to an experience of the divine that is comfort and love cannot be denied, especially once one begins to talk to those who receive such transcendent signals and tokens. As is often the case, those distracted by the cares of this world and a casual reductionism into which they expect God to neatly fit are skeptical and even scornful of the experiences. They are often coupled with intense spiritual depth in the one who receives them and this is not something easily related. As such, it is a personal encounter with the guardian troop that are assigned to one's particular endeavor.

Many times I might have lost courage or succumbed to doubt if it were not for a strategically placed white feather, popping up at just the moment of decision, that let me know I was not left or forsaken, but that God had set a sturdy guard around my soul and that He knew the path my feet would take and the form my thoughts would tend to. So it is objective and rational and even scientific as I can be and often am, I still find there to be much to recommend this love letter from heaven as a genuine and bone fide experience of the numinous and divine as it goes about the mundane task of protecting us and preventing harm to us. It is an encouragement to those who know the meaning of it, and it does no harm to anyone else. We have a saying: "as light as a feather." Yet out of this seeming inconsequentiality, God is provoking faith and courage and steadfastness, and for that reason I dare not dismiss it.

Paul David Radford-Hancock

****

I was having a very bad day one day as I had been denied entrance to a certain health study and dental problems were whacking me out. Life wasn't going how I wanted it to go, and it wasn't moving fast enough. There were some racial problems I was observing where the enemy was trying to create tension—both in the nation and in the church, and it disturbed me. I was at the bathroom mirror getting ready to go somewhere and I told the Lord, "Just talk to me. I know you love us all and that you made us all different colors--please talk to me about it. I want joy; it's in the morning Lord, and I need your joy right now." All of a sudden to the right of me up in the mirror first a white feather pops out and then a black one. They were at least an inch long and they did a dance as they came down together—I watched them fall without trying to catch them, and because of the way my bathroom mirrors are set up I had this three-dimensional view as they fell. I cried, because He does loves us, and we all are one. The black was the blackest black I have ever seen— it was almost blue it was so black. I kept the feathers and store them on my dresser.

Cynthia Palmatier

****

One of the most common questions I hear about the heavenly feathers, and with any similar manifestation, is "What is the point?" Some who ask this are genuine seekers who want greater understanding but have reservations. Others are scoffers who prefer to stand back and mock the things of God with no intention to glean deeper insight into His purposes.

Still others are so filled with awe at what God is doing that they want to soak up everything they can about the subject. This book is geared primarily toward those in awe and wonder, and also for the seekers, as I will attempt to explain, to the best of the revelation and understanding I have at this time, what God is saying and doing through this miracle manifestation.

Feathers are found in a number of places in the Bible, and they suggest the presence of a being with wings, which from a spiritual perspective speaks of angels. It can also refer to the Holy Spirit who appears at times in the form or likeness of a dove. Genesis 1:1-2 says, "In the beginning God created the heavens and the earth. Now the earth was formless and empty, darkness was over the surface of the deep, and the Spirit of God was hovering over the waters" (Strong). The word *hover* in that passage is the Hebrew word *rachaph* which means to brood or hover or flutter softly. In this passage Holy Spirit is represented clearly as a bird hovering over the waters of creation. In fact, my wife pointed out that it's entirely possible the feathers come not from angels, but from Holy Spirit.

The first thing feathers point to is the presence of creative power that is active and ready to accomplish things. This fluttering imagery speaks of potential energy which is stored and waiting to explode out, but this passage is not just suggestive of an energy release like an explosion. Rather, it gives the picture of frequencies being released, as fluttering or hovering represents a steady, rhythmic undulation that

changes the atmosphere around it. Reverend Kenneth
Tanner, a writer for the *Huffington Post*, puts it this way in his
blog, "If God were to stop speaking we would cease to exist
but these Three Who are One are speaking still and now their
Creation is full of language, sings back the divine song it has
learned, whether humans are paying much attention or not.
The Song that sang us into existence is a mystery of self-
sacrificial Love on which rests the foundation of Earth as it
hangs in space" (Tanner). In *The Songlines* Bruce Chatwin
explained that in some ancient belief traditions, such as
Australian aborigines, the common understanding is that
creation was *sung* into existence, which is in keeping with this
image of undulating frequencies (14-15).

In Scripture, Hebrews 1:3s says, "The Son is the radiance
of God's glory and the exact representation of his being,
sustaining all things by his powerful word." The key portion
of this verse which relates to creation and creative energy, and
again to why feathers can represent creative power, has to do
with the part that says "sustaining all things by his powerful
word." To sustain something is to keep it alive on an ongoing
basis. Power, whether electricity or any other kind, when
broken down into its smallest form, beyond even the
subatomic level, is pure energy. A word is something that is
spoken forth, but the nature of words are that they are made
by vibrating vocal chords in such a way as to create a
frequency. If we put it all together, the verse means that God
sustains all of creation by the ongoing frequency and energy
that is released as He verbalizes, which is either talking or

singing. It would not be wrong to claim that God sang the world into existence.

As feathers are a physical sign that point to that creative frequency, we can understand that one of the messages that feathers present to us is that of creative power. This could signify creation in the more artistic sense of creating a work of art or designing or inventing something, or it could speak to a more literal version where we speak things into existence by faith, but regardless of the form that creative power manifests, when feathers appear there is an openness in the atmosphere to tap into a creative flow. As we recognize this sign for what it is, we can better take advantage of that energy when it comes flowing our way.

The second thing feathers point to when they appear is a time of preparation and birthing of new things. In the same way that a hen broods over chicks, the feathers point to a time of watchfulness and protection over something when it is not quite ready to spring forth. At that time the spiritual atmosphere is changing but has not yet reached the tipping point of breakthrough. The message is one of continued prayer, continuing to persevere in what we are doing and to stay the course because the spiritual momentum is building and new things are getting ready to break out. It could also be a sign related to something in the natural—that a project or endeavor we have been working on is almost to the point of coming into being, but that it needs attention to bring it to fulfillment. There are nine different passages in the Bible that refer to there being a "set time" for things. The number nine, in a variety of different belief systems including the Bible, represents finality or completion. The idea that there is a set time for things to be brought to completion is represented Biblically, and the feather is both a sign of this reality, and an encouragement to us to persevere through any difficulties along the way until we reach that completion point.

The third message of the feathers goes hand in hand with the second, which is that of entering a time of refreshing, sustenance, and renewal. Isaiah 40:31 states, "Those who hope in the Lord will renew their strength. They will soar on wings like eagles; they will run and not grow weary, they will walk and not be faint." When feathers appear, it can speak to an opportunity to renew one's strength and energy. When one is preparing to birth something new, it is important to take time to refresh and renew to be prepared for the journey ahead. If creative power has been flowing and new things are coming forth, a feather can appear at the right moment to signal a need to self-rejuvenate, as what will come next is a launching into the new.

The fourth message the feathers bring us is that their appearance is indicative both of warfare and divine protection in the midst of spiritual battles, as well as the struggles and battles in life. If we consider that the Bible speaks a number of times of wings, which are a conglomeration of linked feathers, we see a greater context for the feathers and their subsequent meaning. Psalm 91:1-8 says,

> Whoever dwells in the shelter of the Most High will rest in the shadow of the Almighty. I will say of the

Lord, 'He is my refuge and my fortress, my God, in whom I trust.' Surely he will save you from the fowler's snare and from the deadly pestilence. He will cover you with his feathers, and under his wings you will find refuge; his faithfulness will be your shield and rampart. You will not fear the terror of night, nor the arrow that flies by day, nor the pestilence that stalks in the darkness, nor the plague that destroys at midday. A thousand may fall at your side, ten thousand at your right hand, but it will not come near you. You will only observe with your eyes and see the punishment of the wicked.

Psalm 34:7 also says, "For the angel of the LORD is a guard; he surrounds and defends all who fear him." All of this demonstrates to us that scripturally, feathers are a form of armor and a shield to us, and the above verses demonstrate that like a mother bird caring for its offspring, our Heavenly Father will cover and protect us in much the same way, providing an impenetrable refuge for us to find protection. No matter how difficult our struggles or battles in life and no matter how hard the enemy tries to come against us, we can always find a place of safety with our Father and amidst the protection of the angelic host.

Psalm 64:13 speaks of this armor and protection further: "Even while you sleep among the sheep pens, the wings of my dove are sheathed with silver, its feathers with shining gold." This verse offers imagery that shows the dove protecting the sleeping sheep, but while a dove might not seem like a vicious protector, this one's feathers are sheathed in metal and are presumably razor-sharp. In context, the entirety of Psalm 64, speaks of the Lord going before the armies and scattering his enemies to ensure victory for His chosen ones. The dove's armor of silver and gold is much like one might imagine a King's armor to be adorned with. In this case, the sheep are sleeping soundly and peacefully because they are completely protected. Additional verses that speak of wings and feathers as shelter and protection are Ruth 2:12, Psalm 17:8, 36:7, 57:1, 61:4, Matthew 23:37, and Luke 13:34.

While part of the meaning of the feathers is that God will protect us, there is another aspect of the meaning of feathers for protection that speaks of angels warring on our behalf. My wife and I once knew a couple who were under significant pressure from the demonic realms, and at one point the husband got in a car accident that injured him and could have killed him. Around this time, they found a large pile of feathers that appeared in their home, and the revelation the Lord gave them at the time was that these feathers had fallen off of angels during warfare. Think about it—if multiple winged, feathered beings are swinging swords at each other, at some point some feathers are going to get hacked off! In this case, the feathers manifested in the physical realm to the point that the couple filled multiple plastic containers with them.

This brings us to the fifth message of the feathers. There is a literal war in the spirit realm around us, but it is often hard to remain conscious of this fighting as we go through the day-to-day happenings of our lives. One aspect of the supernatural manifestation of feathers is that it is meant to remind us to shift our focus heavenward. Jesus said that we are to pray for God's will to be done "On earth as it is in heaven." This happens more easily and often when we focus our hearts and minds on things heavenly. The feathers are a simple reminder of the invisible spiritual activity occurring all around us.

A sixth aspect of the feathers is relational in nature. Quite often when we engage the angels in prayer, conversation, and during times of worship, we find feathers begin to appear— usually only one or two, but enough to let us know that what we are doing is effective. I should clarify here—when I say we engage the angels in worship, I do not mean that we worship angels. Colossians 2:8 says, "Do not let anyone who delights in false humility and the worship of angels disqualify you. Such a person also goes into great detail about what they have seen; they are puffed up with idle notions by their unspiritual mind." Angels are spirits who minister to us, who can be our friends and protectors, and who can encourage and help us in our daily lives as well as to secure salvation, but we are not to worship them. That right and honor is reserved for the Creator, our Heavenly Father, who loves us more than life itself—the one who loved us so much that He chose to sacrifice himself on our behalf to set us free from the powers of death, sin, and darkness.

With that disclaimer in place, relationships with angels remains a key part of this whole miracle-business and is often overlooked. Angels have feelings and thoughts much like a human. They can feel pain and pleasure like we do, but currently have bodies that are far superior to ours. However, given that God has created angels to be relational as He has with us, when we pay attention to angels, we will find that they interact more with us—it's a two way street. Thus, as we do this we may find that feathers appear as physical confirmation to us that our spiritual interaction is not imagined but instead is quite real—and when we start to work more purposefully with angels, feathers are the least of the things we can expect to see.

To illustrate this point, I will share a story. When my wife and I drove six hours to meet our friends in Coeur D'Alene, we talked and enjoyed spending time together, but we also spent some time in prayer and planning some ministry and writing related things. At one point I became conscious of an angel who was flying right in front of the truck as I drove. I shared this with her and we began to pray and both speak to the angel as well have it share with us what it was there to accomplish. The more we prayed and engaged it, the more occurred. More angels either appeared or we simply became aware of those that were already present. As we did this, two or three small, wispy white feathers appeared and floated around inside of the truck cab, confirming our encounter with them. We swiftly entered a time of strong intercession over our lives and our future, and God gave us some clear direction—all because we became aware of the presence of angels and began to engage them.

The seventh message of the feathers is in regards to healing. As I mentioned in the beginning of this chapter, the feathers speak of creative power, and healing is one manifestation of that creative energy, but I feel this is significant enough to note as a separate message of the feathers. The connection between the appearance of feathers and the story that took place at the Pool of Bethesda is clear in John 5:2-4 where it states, "Now there is in Jerusalem near the Sheep Gate a pool, which in Aramaic is called Bethesda and which is surrounded by five covered colonnades. Here a great number of disabled people used to lie—the blind, the lame, the paralyzed. From time to time an angel of the Lord would come down and stir up the waters. The first one into the pool after each such disturbance would be cured of whatever disease they had." Bethesda means "house of mercy" or "house of kindness," and this pool was prophetically named because healing is a manifestation of God's kindness and mercy. For whatever reason, this pool had an angel that was assigned to it, and it would stir the waters at specific moments—much like the set times mentioned earlier.

Angels have a strong association with healing, and the feathers represent their involvement in the healing process. Jesus used them to bring healing as well, as illustrated in Luke 7:1-10 (also in Matthew 8:5-9):

> When Jesus had finished saying all this to the people who were listening, he entered Capernaum. There a centurion's servant, whom his master valued highly, was sick and about to die. The centurion heard

of Jesus and sent some elders of the Jews to him, asking him to come and heal his servant. When they came to Jesus, they pleaded earnestly with him, 'This man deserves to have you do this, because he loves our nation and has built our synagogue.' So Jesus went with them.

He was not far from the house when the centurion sent friends to say to him: 'Lord, don't trouble yourself, for I do not deserve to have you come under my roof. That is why I did not even consider myself worthy to come to you. But say the word, and my servant will be healed. For I myself am a man under authority, with soldiers under me. I tell this one, 'Go,' and he goes; and that one, 'Come,' and he comes. I say to my servant, 'Do this,' and he does it.'

When Jesus heard this, he was amazed at him, and turning to the crowd following him, he said, 'I tell you, I have not found such great faith even in Israel.' Then the men who had been sent returned to the house and found the servant well.

Jesus and the centurion both knew that Jesus didn't need to go in person to heal the centurion's servant. As the centurion sent in a message through some friends, he understood that Jesus had angels under his authority, and much like the soldiers under the centurion's command, all Jesus had to do was send his celestial servants to carry out what he commanded and it would be so. Likewise, the angel at the pool of Bethesda had been tasked with a mission, albeit a strange one, to heal the first person who got into the whirlpool when he stirred up the waters. One of the messages of the feathers is about healing, and about a special "now-moment" for that healing. When feathers appear, it may be a good time to pray for those who need physical or emotional healing, and it can be a sign that healing is taking place and prayers are being answered if they appear during or after a time when prayer for healing has occurred.

The eighth purpose of the feathers is to help us cultivate miracles. When feathers appear out of thin air, a shift starts to take place in our minds. When we experience the miraculous, our minds renew—it doesn't matter if a feather disappears or remains—the event changes our thinking. It is possible to explain away even the most marvelous of miracles through great effort and mental gymnastics, but if one is honest in their own reasoning, the end explanation for miracles will lead them to a greater appreciation for God's hand at work and will invariably shift their thoughts toward a higher plane of spiritual reality, which invites even more of the miraculous in. Jesus instructed his disciples to pray that God's will would be done "On earth as it is in heaven" (Matthew 6:10), and the feathers are a training tool God uses to transform our belief systems about what is possible and impossible so that we are better equipped to manifest miracles.

The ninth message of the feathers is far simpler than the others although in some ways it sums the rest of them up. Feathers from heaven are a symbol of God's love for us. Sending us angels, watching over and protecting us, giving us new strength and creative power to do new things and bringing healing are all ways that God demonstrates His love for us. If there is only a single message that one remembers from this book and what the feathers mean, let it speak of God's goodness and love, of His mercy and kindness, and let it be remembered that when a feather appears, God is smiling down upon us, knows what is going on in our lives, and is ready to shower us with an abundance of grace, favor, and blessings.

Chapter 3

Discernment and Deception

My son was about six when he asked me, "What is God like, mommy?" I was a bit taken aback. I did not want cliché answers. I raised him to understand what I told him about heaven as my soul cried out with a quick "Help, Father". I looked up and this fluffy feather drifted down from midair. Instantly we likened God to a feather, soft and gentle, light and calm. I wondered, and still do, how my duvet fluff could have shot up such a big feather . . . well formed, dense and pure white.

Anny Ruch

****

My husband and I had swirling pillars of large white feathers about five feet above our heads. He saw mine and pointed for me to look up and see them and I told him he had the same thing over his head! It was during a very difficult time in our lives and we were both very encouraged!

Lisa Deming

****

About 6 years ago, I had been unemployed for a long time and was praying as I drove. Suddenly I saw a huge white feather float down in front of my car! I got a job soon after that. Also after having been to Michael King's home, where we found gems from heaven, the next morning I was having some doubts and asked God to confirm the gems were really from Him. I stepped out of my car and about two feet in front of me was a beautiful white feather! Settled it for me! On January 20th of this year (2016), I had just been to the doctor who told me I had shingles, and that was hard. As I used the restroom after the appointment, I hung my car keys on the hook on the door. When I retrieved them there was a 2" feather stuck through the keyring, which was such an encouragement!!

Irmgard Lam

****

One of the most disappointing things about the supernatural are the heresy-hunters. Often ministers of the gospel themselves, they have entire websites devoted to pointing the finger at other brothers and sisters in the body of Christ, who they believe are leading the world deep into deception. I can't presume to know what these self-appointed deception-monitors believe, but they seem to feel it is their duty to denounce anyone and everyone who operates in signs, wonders, and miracles. It would be no surprise to me if my name is eventually added to that list for having the gall to write such books as this one. In spite of the poor character the moderators of these types of websites tend to display, they do have one thing right—we would be wise to discern accurately the spiritual happenings in our lives. While an extremely enjoyable miracle, feathers from heaven are no different in this regard.

If we consider that demons are fallen angels, then in theory, demons should be able to produce feathers as well. 2 Corinthians 11:14 says, "And no wonder, for Satan himself masquerades as an angel of light." If fallen angels can pretend to be non-fallen angels, then feathers appearing, in and of themselves, are not a guarantee that angelic activity is afoot, but it most often is. I suggest it is extremely uncommon for demons to pop feathers out, as they tend to thrive on hiding in the shadows and on not making their presence known. 1 John 4:1 gives us this advice, "Dear friends, do not believe every spirit, but test the spirits to see whether they are from God, because many false prophets have gone out into the world." It is good to be aware that angels don't have a corner on the feather-market, so we simply must use discernment at all times and always seek to differentiate and understand whom we are dealing with before deciding one way or the other—as to whether something is life-giving or not.

It can be very confusing when wanting to learn more about this subject, because there are actually a wide variety of internet resources on supernatural feathers. Most commonly, one will find websites that talk about angel guides and that feathers are one of the most common sign of angelic presence. Other sites speak about ancestors and how feathers are a sign of our loved ones speaking to us from across the grave and that when we find angel feathers, it signifies that our recently departed loved ones have successfully crossed over to the afterlife. All of these views are based on someone's perspective and can further muddy the waters when we want to discern whether something is from God or not.

While most Christians who believe that feathers appear from heaven think it's a Christian phenomenon, as mentioned above, people of other belief systems experience them as well. There could be a number of reasons for this, and the goal of this chapter is to look at the risks of being led into deception and how we can discern where this manifestation is coming from. The term "deception" is readily bandied around when discussing miracles, and it is possibly one of the things that annoys me the most—everyone is so afraid of getting deceived that they are prone to run in fear regardless of whether it is needed or not. I also suggest that running in fear is rarely an appropriate action when dealing with the spiritual realm or miraculous signs.

The biggest deception I believe people can get into with this miraculous manifestation is the deception of fear. When we start to get afraid that we are going to be deceived, that is when the enemy has us right where he wants us. Fear is the gateway to all sorts of problems, so even if we decide to proceed with caution in some manner, asking God to give us confirmation and guidance, that doesn't necessarily make us "doubters" but makes us people who want to walk wisely. My wife has had past experiences with some really wonky people so she tends to be very cautious in most spiritual situations where I am usually more adventurous with a "let's see what happens" attitude. Proverbs 11:14 says that, "For lack of guidance a nation falls, but victory is won through many advisers." When having concerns or doubts about something, we shouldn't immediately go to the knee-jerk fear reaction. Instead, if we take some time to seek wise counsel and even talk to people we know will have different perspectives, we will come to a much clearer understanding. I have had people approach me over social media because they simply didn't have anyone else in their sphere of influence with a similar perspective. It's not that they were going to take my word over everyone else's, but they wanted to hear from a voice that was different from the input they normally received and they felt I was a safe option to turn to. It's perfectly okay to go through a process and think things out—we don't have to arrive at answers instantly with most things, and God isn't going to penalize us for trying to be wise as we walk things out—after all, He is the Spirit of Wisdom (Isaiah 11:2).

The word "deceive" means to delude or mislead by way of false appearance or the false appearing as though it were true. The word comes ultimately from the Latin word decipere, which essentially means to ensnare or take away [one's freedom] ("Deceive"). When this word is used in religious circles, it is typically meant to denigrate someone and show that they have fallen away from the pre-ordained path of appropriate beliefs as ordained by a higher religious body. More often than not, however, the word basically gets used in any situation where someone's belief departs enough from our own where we feel that person holding that belief is somehow a threat, and we label them accordingly. Ideas aren't harmful in and of themselves. Simply hearing an idea we disagree with isn't going to damn our mortal souls for eternity, so the first step in any discernment process is to drop the fear level down a few thousand notches. The wonderful thing about the uninhibited flow of ideas among people is that only those who want to control others feel a need to stop free thought.

The first thing I look at when I think about the idea of being deceived is that every single person on the earth is not only at risk for errors in their beliefs, but all of us could be considered deceived already, in that every one of us has at least one or two errors in our beliefs—and I'd be willing to bet that we each have more than just a couple. While I believe it is wise to make good use of discernment, I start out by discussing this because I want us to be able to look at this concept freely without fearing that demons are going to attack or invade us somehow just by looking at ideas that might be uncommon or outside of the mainstream.

Feathers appearing from heaven could be considered a form of deception by some—a "lying sign" as some translations of the Bible call it. If something is deceptive, it is meant to mislead, and in this case, the assumption is that it is meant to lead us away from God. In reality, being misled in a spiritual sense is only a major problem long-term when people turn away from what God is doing. God is committed to bringing each of us into a transformative understanding of His love, which in turn changes our hearts and minds to reflect that love more and more. Even if we mess up here and there along the way, God has already promised to finish the job He started, as He says in Philippians 1:6, ". . . being confident of this, that he who began a good work in you will carry it on to completion until the day of Christ Jesus." God doesn't do things halfway, and He is faithful to do what He says He will do. Even when someone becomes misled about something, God will always draw them back. I often say, "God's ability to keep me is greater than the enemy's ability to deceive me." I believe we must live in a place of trust where we extend our faith actively toward God, believing that He will keep us. I have found in my own life that as I have done this, truth and clarity are what I receive.

In regards to so-called "lying signs", we must remember that the Bible is full of the miraculous. The word "sign(s)" appears 80 times, "miracle(s)" appears 30 times, and "wonder(s)" appears 109 times. The vast majority of the Bible either recounts supernatural events or is a record of God speaking supernaturally to people. As a whole, it should be normal to expect that unexpected things will happen because God is a creative God who likes doing new things. While His nature doesn't change (Hebrews 13:8 says "Jesus Christ is the same yesterday and today and forever."), God may choose to do new things; the book of Isaiah mentions this multiple times:

"See, the former things have taken place, and new things I declare; before they spring into being I announce them to you. (Isaiah 42:9)"

"See, I am doing a new thing! Now it springs up; do you not perceive it? I am making a way in the wilderness and streams in the wasteland" (Isaiah 43:19).

"You have heard these things; look at them all. Will you not admit them? "From now on I will tell you of new things, of hidden things unknown to you" (Isaiah 48:6).

"See, I will create new heavens and a new earth. The former things will not be remembered, nor will they come to mind" (Isaiah 65:17).

God isn't changing who He is or redefining His nature by doing new things. Instead, God is a creator and enjoys changing things and making things new. Amos 3:7 says, "Surely the Sovereign Lord does nothing without revealing his plan to his servants the prophets. When God does anything new He shows His people what He is doing, so it is perfectly natural that we should not only hear about new things God is doing, but experience them as well.

I share this because it is important that we have a foundational understanding that it is entirely scriptural to have signs, wonders, and miracles occur in our lives, and also for God to do new things that may or may not be written explicitly in Biblical text. While it would be nice if there was an easy proof-text that says something like "Yea, verily, I shalt send thee feathers from the wings of angels and thou shalt useth it for thine bedding-eth" there simply isn't one. Nevertheless, for those who feel something must be included in the scriptures for God to do it (as though the Bible binds and limits God instead of revealing Him) there are sufficient principles found in scripture to make room for this phenomenon, and many others. Feathers from heaven are a sign pointing to a number of things, as discussed in the previous chapter.

Keeping all this in mind, we still want to use wisdom and attempt to discern what spirits are behind the feathers simply because angels aren't the only spirits out there who can make things appear. Demons have been understood for centuries to be fallen angels who have cut themselves off (or have been cut off) from God as a power source, but rearranging atoms to appear in the shape of a feather isn't above their capabilities either. That said, angels are the most likely source, if for no other reason than God is creative and anything creative is more likely to be from God than not. There is a book by the title of *All Truth is God's Truth* which in summary says just that—truth is only derived from God, even if it comes from the mouth of a satanist, because Satan is the father of lies and the truth is not in him (John 8:44).

Some people believe ancestors and those who have died send feathers as a message to people here on earth. That's possible, but I'm not sure where that idea comes from and I have no way of proving or disproving the notion. Hebrews 12:1 states that we are surrounded by a cloud of witnesses, referring to people who have already died. In Mark 12:27 Jesus explains to the Pharisees that, "He is not the God of the dead, but of the living. You are badly mistaken!" This same comment is found in Matthew 22:32 and Luke 20:38, the latter of which says it a bit differently, "He is not the God of the dead, but of the living, for to him all are alive." If all are alive, then it is entirely plausible that there could be some sort of God-ordained interaction between those who have gone to Heaven before us. The Old Testament hints at this possibility as well when it speaks of the men in white linen. The Bible doesn't specify clearly whether these men are humans or angels specifically, but according to *Strong's Concordance,* the Hebrew word *iysh* which is used to describe them literally means "man" whereas in most instances when it is referring to an angel it will use the Hebrew word *malak* denoting a representative or messenger. Each time an angel appears the word *malak* is used, and when it refers to a man it will either say *iysh* or *enowsh* which basically means a mortal/human, with the exception of Genesis 18 and 19, where in Genesis 18 the men who visit Abraham are referred to as *enowsh,* mortal men, but in Chapter 19 when they visit Lot they are referred to as *malak,* messenger (Strong). Since this makes things as clear as mud, we essentially can conclude that scripturally speaking, the Bible just isn't clear. In other words, it is entirely possible that throughout the Bible God sent actual men from heaven to interact with men on earth. While this doesn't prove one way or the other whether the deceased can send feathers from heaven, it does suggest that there's a lot more going on in the spirit realm than we have any clue, and it's at least a possibility that we cannot disprove. Regardless of whether it's angels or people sending the feathers, as long as the source is heavenly, we can enjoy them freely. With that said, I still personally find it most plausible that feathers would appear from angels, as angels can have wings and humans don't.

When we want to discern something, there are only two real methods. The first is by the physical fruit of the manifestation. The second is via spiritual perception. Spiritual perception is very useful, and while someone else may respond and follow that personal perception, it is mostly only appropriate for personal decision-making or in a group who has seen that perception be consistently accurate over time. Perception differs from person to person, but when multiple people agree on a thing, generally a consensus in that group is pretty reasonable. Sometimes one person will feel something is "off" when many others feel it is just fine. There are a few reasons for this—one being that everyone is in deception, and the other being that it's perfectly fine for most people but for whatever reason, for that individual it is not. The danger of trying to tell everyone else that they are wrong when one person has that "off" feeling is that it's a personal perception, so there is no hard factual data to prove to everyone who is right. The good news? God is good at taking care of his own people and working all things for good. If things do go awry, God will work that out too. If someone has a feeling that something is right or wrong, it is usually best to follow that feeling and trust that God will show the way.

To discern the physical fruit of a manifestation requires one to look at the people who are engaging that manifestation and see what they have experienced. We cover personal testimonies in Chapter 5, but I want to look at the notion of fruit-testing a bit more in this chapter first. The real issue with deception is when people turn away from God and what He is doing. When people only fall more in love with God, only praise His goodness even more, and become more likely to engage the supernatural realms around them as God reveals it to them, that doesn't sound like someone who is deceived. It sounds like someone whose eyes are being opened to a greater measure of what God is doing in the earth, and whose heart is being opened further toward Him. I have run into all sorts of people who find the feathers to be a "demonic deception" but I simply have not experienced or witnessed any of the things I would expect to see from highly deceived people who are turning away from God and His plans or purposes.

While some argue that heavenly feathers are a distraction from telling others about Jesus, these individuals are rarely running themselves ragged finding new effective evangelistic outlets, so it seems rather hypocritical. On the other hand, I find that unique miracles such as feathers appearing create for cool opportunities to share about God with others. I do it often when I see feathers appear at work or in other public places. All I have to do is announce "oh—a feather just appeared. Do you see it?" as I point to the feather floating along. Right there I have opened up a conversation and can see where it leads. Feathers are no more or less a distraction than is TV, work, or personal belongings, and anything can be a distraction if we let it. That kind of flawed logic is the sort of thing that leads groups such as the Amish to live as they do in an attempt to be "in the world but not of it" when in reality they have simply traded a 21st century world for a 19th century one with all the same potential for distraction.

How can we know for sure that feathers are from heaven? There is sufficient scriptural backing, the fruit of the manifestation is fairly consistently positive, and there is little to be gained by demons doing it when people only praise God louder as a result. In other words, there isn't all that much room for the feathers to be a demonic artifice.

Even with that in mind, I am probably more of a skeptic than one might typically expect when it comes to materials appearing from the air, especially with feathers. I believe that discussing the false is just as important at looking at why I believe the feather manifestation is legitimate because I believe in transparency. While I value miracles highly, and I enjoy feathers greatly, I also don't like stupidity. If we have a feather pillow and a feather blanket on our bed, when a single feather appears on the floor of the bedroom right next to the bed, or on the bed itself, I generally assume it was from the pillow or blanket. Why? Because it's the most obvious source. We also have chickens. If I find a colored feather in the yard, or even on the floor of the house looking a bit muddy—like my shoes might have tracked this sad looking excuse for a feather in from outside, I tend to believe it comes from one of our chickens, not an angel, especially when the colors match. Why? Because it's the most obvious source.

One of the reasons some skeptics are skeptical is precisely because in our excitement to experience miracles we can overdo things. I recall a story a friend told me where he was at a conference and he saw a group of people by the stage getting all excited because gold dust and feathers were appearing on them. He took about six seconds to look around and observed that someone was standing on stage practically on top of them waving a flag that had both golden glitter and feathers on it. He was a bit perturbed because it seemed to him that these people had left all reason at the door in their excitement, as the source seemed somewhat obvious to him.

For some it may seem that I am trying to "kill their faith" when I don't think a feather on top of my feather-blanket is from heaven, but I simply want to maintain the legitimacy of the miracle and I prefer to avoid reasons for reproach when possible. Back in 2013 when my wife and I hosted gem parties, and even when I had personally witnessed thousands appear, when people would tell me the ministers present were planting gems, I didn't just take their word for that they were being planted, and neither did I assume that no one was planting them either—I looked for myself and actively observed.

It isn't hard to look around and find a potential source or lack thereof for most supernatural manifestations. If oil starts pooling in the kitchen, I'm likely to look for the nearby olive oil bottle to see if it spilled. If it starts pooling on my bedroom wall, I'm likely to assume it's from heaven. If gold dust appears on my arms, well, I don't use sparkly makeup, but I know women who do, so if I see what I call "sparklies" on women, I usually ask them first if they wear glitter-makeup or glitter-lotion. If they don't, then I tell them about the sparklies they have on them, and they are usually blessed. If they do, I just let them know I noticed, and thought it was pretty, and they are usually blessed by the compliment too.

In closing, I believe one of the biggest things missing in the discernment game is grace. I think that as we all learn to grow in this area, we have to start by giving it lavishly to one another. We all mess up. We all make mistakes. In the midst of that, we all have opportunities for growth. If we have concerns, when we talk to someone privately and quietly we extend mercy and give them room to grow. If we publicly denounce them as a knee-jerk reaction without speaking to them privately we cut off any grace toward that person, which does two things. First, we are usually not walking in love at that point and are simply the demonic hand of judgment toward them. Second, we reap what we sow, which means we are essentially cutting off grace toward ourselves and inviting judgments from others upon our lives as well. We don't necessarily have to agree with one another about the feathers miracle, but a demonstration of good character and actively extending mercy toward one another goes a long way, especially if we believe someone is in error. When we break down lines of communication we are less able to speak into someone else's life as they simply don't allow us access. At the same time, it's entirely possible that we could be the one who is wrong in any given situation, and if we habitually extend kindness to others, being slow to judge, we are more likely to find that same favor extended toward us in return.

Chapter 4
Ruffled Feathers

I was feeling kind of discouraged because of my fractured elbow and my hand not being able to be used. I was talking to the Lord and I walked into the bathroom and there was this beautiful white feather. I knew it wasn't there before because it was in the upstairs bathroom and the windows weren't open or anything. It just was a really beautiful touch of love from the Lord and I got so excited. I put it up on the windowsill and it's still there.

On another occasion a couple of weeks ago I found a beautiful white feather. I opened the front door and there it was, right in front of the door. There must have been an angel standing in front of the door because I don't have many birds around there with white feathers, and it's a pristine, clean white.

Judy Hope

****

During worship a few weeks ago I watched a feather float down from the ceiling and land on an aisle chair a couple rows in front of me. I wanted so bad to dash up there and retrieve it before it was sat on! During the altar call at the end of service four people came forward which has never happened in years of going there. It seemed proof to me of an angel sent to minister in that service!

Jonelle Hunt

****

I am blessed to know there are others who "play with God as a Father". God can do this with anything—feathers, clovers, money, messages He sends us in dreams, visions, and even road signs. He created the substance of which all things are created, as "in Him and through Him all things hold together," so why not feathers, or gems, or anything else?

I believe there is a bigger reason and picture behind what the Lord is doing with feathers and gems. Feathers and gems are not "life threatening" faith issues—rather they are child-like in the seeking like I go hunting for clovers. The Lord once told me that the only reason I find my 4, 5, and 6 leaf clovers is because I ask him for them and then look for them. It has helped me to get to a place where I stay in peace and encouragement, knowing the Lord is there and answering my heart cries even with things that others find meaningless. Anyone in Tennessee can find 4-leaf clovers, but the 5 and 6 leaf clovers takes God creating from the earth, growing plants to respond to my request. These are all little ways God expands our child-like faith.

Rachel Irene Ciardi

****

While in the last chapter we discussed the heresy-hunters—people who take it upon themselves to track down every deception they can find and announce it to the world; that group of people can often be handled by completely ignoring them. Hard on their heels, however, are a second group of people who are equally frustrating—the marginalizers. It is hard to discuss the supernatural without someone who takes offense at the miracle in question and who then tries to marginalize, minimize, or otherwise downplay its significance. I cannot count the number of times I have heard people make ignorant statements like, "Why would God send _____ (insert name of miracle) when there are starving children in _____ (insert country name), when people groups are being persecuted, there are homeless in the street, people need healing, _____ (insert additional problems here), etc. This is one of the most predictable responses (and possibly the most annoying) because it attempts to invalidate the miraculous by throwing unrelated problems at it as though the miracle in question is somehow expected to produce world peace, end pollution and child slavery, cure cancer, and increase exports from third world countries by 40%.

This is the type of response the Pharisees gave Jesus whenever he did miracles among them. "But it's the Sabbath—who said you can heal on the Sabbath?" "Whose sin caused him to be born blind—his or his parents'?" "Who gave you the authority to forgive his sins?" If we can't stop you from doing miracles, and we can't explain the miracles within our tiny religious box, then we need to question them so far into the ground that they won't dare pop their head out of the groundhog hole until spring. There are so many different things that ruffle people's feathers that I'm sure we will miss some, but this chapter is an attempt to address some of the common objections related to the feather-miracle that don't fit neatly into the discernment category.

As mentioned above, the common marginalization response is to find a list of things the miracle doesn't solve, then use that list as ammunition to discredit or somehow invalidate the miracle. In the end, the comments that marginalize miracles by pointing to other problems are a red herring—they have literally nothing to do with the miracle at all and simply divert attention from the matter at hand. The question itself is a complete distraction. It is easy to go around complaining about what other people are doing, seeing, experiencing, etc. and why either God wouldn't or shouldn't, and why we are too focused on this to accomplish that, or whatever, but it's all missing the point. There are numerous problems with this concept, so let us take a look at a few of the most common questions the marginalizers tend to throw out when they attack:

- "How does this help promote the Gospel?"

  I challenge a single person to come up with a "ministry" reason that Jesus walked on water. The disciples were in the middle of the lake at night in the middle of a storm, and the text explicitly states that

Jesus wasn't planning on stopping for them (Mark 6:48). In other words, he was either out for a joy-walk, which is probably the case, or he was just trying to shorten the distance between points to get somewhere on time, which is unlikely since he could have simply teleported like he did with the disciples right after he got into the boat a short time later (John 6:21). Contrary to popular belief, not everything one does that has the stamp of spirituality on it has to advance ministry or preach the gospel. Sure, one of the wonderful things about miracles are the opportunity they bring to share God's love with people, but that's not the only thing that miracles do. Miracles can increase faith, solve problems, create favor, and much more. The good news that God isn't counting our sin against us and we no longer have to die is fantastic news, but it's not the *only* news.

- "How can you waste time on this miracle when there are: homeless; starving children; wars; slavery; etc.?"

    Simple: Given the vast resources of our Heavenly Father, I might actually be able to do both. Counter-question: How come so many churches have paid for construction of a "coffee bar" inside the church when it doesn't help starving children in Africa? How much of your budget is spent at the local coffee shop feeding your caffeine addiction with five-dollar cups of coffee? How does THAT help starving African children? People who ask this question are usually just as inconsistent with their own spirituality as they are accusing the other person of. Let's be honest, how much time does it take to observe a feather floating by? Seconds. If they start appearing in quantity one might spend more time than that, but most of the time it only takes a few seconds to acknowledge the miracle and keep going, especially when it happens regularly. In fact, earlier today before writing this chapter, a small feather appeared and I took less than a minute to recognize the feather was there then pray and ask God what He wanted to show me. The instructions I got were to work on this chapter instead of another one I was planning on writing this evening—some really practical guidance that turned out to be extremely helpful. After that, the encounter was over. I'm not sure how many lepers I could have healed in the sixty seconds I sat in my kitchen wasting time on a feather miracle, but I don't think it would be very many. You see, there just aren't any lepers in my kitchen, so it would have been hard to put that time to better use.

- "How does some [stupid] little feather bring glory to God?"

Let me tell you a little story about a nickel. A number of years back, I watched a short video online where a man was sticking bobby pins to a wall by faith. I saw it and thought "I want to try it!" I grabbed a nickel on the desk in front of me and held it to the wall. As I did so, I immediately felt a jolt of power shoot from my finger up my arm, and at that moment I also felt the nickel adhere to the wall—it stayed put for about five minutes with faith as the only adhesive to hold it in place. I shared that miracle with a number of friends at the time, most of whom were also able to replicate the miracle, and since then I have shared it with many others, most of whom were also able to replicate it either immediately or at a later date. What's the point of this and how does it relate to bringing God glory? The most notable change I observed as a result of sticking coins to walls was that when I prayed for the sick and injured, more of them got healed faster and more frequently. What does a gravity-related miracle have to do with healing the sick? At first glance, nothing. But remember that jolt of power that went up my arm? As I activated my faith, I received an impartation of something from heaven that caused me to be more effective, and that effect has lasted to this day, over five years later. A miracle doesn't have to "make sense" to the rational mind. In fact, God clearly states that he offends our minds on purpose. In 1 Corinthians 1:27 Paul states, "But God chose the foolish things of the world to shame the wise; God chose the weak things of the world to shame the strong." God isn't so worried about everything matching our rational understanding that He won't offend our sensibilities, because He will. I wouldn't be surprised if someday someone has plastic packing material appear supernaturally—not because the person needs to move, but because it's downright ridiculous and sometimes God wants to offend our minds to get at our hearts.

In the midst of the attempts to marginalize miracles, one of the things people often miss are the spiritual nutrients present in the miracles that are designed to enhance our lives. When the feather appeared earlier, what if I hadn't taken the time to stop and listen for God's direction? I certainly wouldn't have written this chapter when I did, and maybe I wouldn't have been successful getting any writing done at all! Believe it or not, it can be pretty easy to miss out on what God wants to do through a miracle, especially if we look at it through the wrong lens. There is a reason Paul instructs us on how we should think: "Finally, brothers and sisters, whatever is true, whatever is noble, whatever is right, whatever is pure, whatever is lovely, whatever is admirable—if anything is excellent or praiseworthy—think about such things" (Philippians 4:8)." When we look at things with the right mindset, we absorb the nutrients from the event. When we don't, we miss out.

One example of this is a conversation I had with a man who informed me that the feathers and gold dust aren't meaningful to him. There's nothing inherently wrong with that and I'm sure many other people feel the same way. In this conversation this man explained that he was wary of the feathers, gems, and the like because he had been warned years before that we are in the end times and many will be deceived by cunning pastors who are filled with deceit and trickery. He explained that prophetic words are more meaningful to him, and that he simply doesn't see physical objects appearing miraculously as being practical. What got me was that he went on to share that he would prefer to see God provide money to pay off student loans and buy food for local families in need. The problem is that in this conversation the man clearly missed the point of the miracles he has seen—that God is demonstrating to him through these signs that there is abundant provision available to meet those very needs—even to the point of seeing money appear supernaturally. While he is busy not wanting these miracles, he doesn't realize they point to a general availability of the things he *does* need and want. In other words, when we turn up our nose at the things God does in our midst, we miss out on the potential blessings those very things can provide. If we allow our faith level to be expanded by gems and feathers and the like, why not apply that newly cultivated faith and extend it to see resources multiply, have bills supernaturally paid and debts cancelled, or even believe for gold, silver, or dollar bills to appear so those financial needs are met. While I understand some people feel a need to be wary, it is possible to be so vigilant that we miss out on the blessings as well. I believe that miracles, like feathers appearing from heaven, are meant to teach us something. These miracles are not just meant to give us handfuls of feathers to make pillows—they are stepping stones to greater dominion in the earth.

To help us reach that greater dominion, God does not hesitate, as I mentioned before, to offend our minds, and often the religious mindsets we have painstakingly developed over time as well. When we have a mental list of what God will and won't do, we can bet that God will find a way to burn the list. What usually comes next is that we refine our list and make a new one, but this time with thick card stock and glitter. When God burns that one, we pull out a fresh piece of colored paper and a gel pen to start over. When that one goes up in flames, we resort to fine sheets of thin, cloth-like paper and calligraphy strokes, not realizing that this entire time God is trying to get us to look at things in a new way instead of doing the same things we have done before using a slightly different method. God wants to draw us deeper—both in relationship with Him and in our role as stewards of creation. Romans 8:19 says it this way, "For the creation waits in eager expectation for the children of God to be revealed." Feathers, gems, and any other supernatural manifestation are a teaching tool to help us grow up in the knowledge and fullness of Him, the Creator, and to manifest His love in the entire cosmos.

As people sit back and complain about the miracles, they are missing out on the great grace that God is extending toward them. And grace, as mentioned in a previous chapter, is one of the key parts that has been missing from this miracle encounter prior to now, and it is little surprise that many manifestations have died out in the past or remained fairly low-key, because instead of honoring one another, we have spent our time criticizing and pointing fingers. What some seem to forget is that as we relate to God and our hearts become more like His, we will naturally want to help the poor, heal the sick, etc. We will do good works simply because it's in our heart to do them, not out of a sense of duty or that we need to stop the "silly miracles" to do the "real work." No, God is big enough that we can have our cake and eat it too. For this reason, and for many others, it is very important that we learn to extend more grace to one another—yes, even to the marginalizers, because Jesus loves and gives grace to them as well, so we should too!

Chapter 5

Feather Stories

While my words and experiences carry value, I believe that God is doing far more with this miracle than just one person can express. To this end I have peppered the book with other people's testimonies, but this whole chapter is a collection of stories—not of the one, but the many—men and women from all over who have witnessed and experienced this extraordinary miracle. These are meant to be an encouragement and to stir your faith, and I pray they draw you deeper into God's heart of love.

****

When I first received the baptism in the Holy Spirit, I would come home from work for lunch so I could praise God. The air always seemed thick with His presence, like syrup and blobs of jello. I felt like there were others there too, angels.

And I found feathers in the house. We had gotten rid of our old feather pillows because they seemed to make me allergic. I think I got rid of all the down stuffed jackets too, so the appearance of feathers was a mystery at first, but these feathers were different. Many of them were long and slender and they never stopped moving. If you found one and picked it up, it seemed like it was dancing. There didn't seem to be much wind inside that old cottage we were staying in at the time, but the feathers wiggled and bowed and waved. They seemed like, if they came off an angel, they were not dead, like old hair, but they were alive and couldn't help but to continue dancing. I used to keep the feathers in little tins that you could get breath mints in. I shared about them with believers, and these people agreed, they had never seen feathers like these before.

Once, we were up in Toronto at the Airport Christian Fellowship, and the anointing was so strong, and we missed some friends who couldn't come and enjoy the revival atmosphere with us. We were praying that something would appear for us to take home with us, and a huge feather appeared right in front of us on a coat or jacket that was laid over the back of a chair. We took it back to our friend as a gift from God.

My wife and I used to make oil for a local healing room and we would prophesy over every little tiny bottle we filled. We were making oil for the rooms, but filling tiny vials also so that people could buy some for a couple of bucks and take it home. It helped us get more oil and essential ingredients and to share the blessing of the oil carrying the presence of God.

We prophesied over every little bottle what the Spirit seemed to be saying, and sometimes it looked like there were little tornadoes, whirlwinds inside the bottles, like they were full of energy and ready to take someone up into heaven like as it happened to Elijah.

We saved angel feathers we found and put them into oil we were consecrating. One day my wife was pouring up some oil for a friend and an angel feather appeared inside a bottle! No one put it there. One moment it wasn't there, and the next moment it was.

Feathers falling at a friend's wedding, during worship, or while making oil always indicated to us that the angels were present, and they were from God, they were good, and they were helping release the power of heaven. It's like gems, glory glitter dust, a sudden electric presence, these things all seem to come in worship or prayer to encourage us that supernatural things are happening, and that God is with us. Sometimes it's just for you, a little sign, a wink from God, that He is watching.

Paul Wilcox

****

Before my husband and I got married we both prayed for Abba and the whole heavenly realm to invade our atmosphere during our wedding. The theme of our wedding was peacock and throughout the entire ceremony we received brightly colored feathers with spotted 'eyes' at the tips. Furthermore, as our minister pronounced our marriage, two feathers (black and white) fell from the atmosphere intertwined in one another. It was shared that black and white are the Jewish wedding colors which was incredible since we had a Jewish inspired wedding. God is SO good!

Hannah Smith

****

My favorite feather story was when I was in Training for Reigning. I didn't want to go but the Lord told me to. I figured that between my Undergraduate and Master's degrees, the latter from Multnomah Bible College, that with all the churches I had been at that made me go through all their classes and schools, I was like, "Really God, do I really need one more school?" I told God I would do it if He really wanted me to, and that I would tell my husband once, but I wasn't going to bring it up again. Right before the school session started, Glenn went online and applied for me, and without having any of the references they usually require, they accepted me in.

During this period, I had a conversation with my senior pastor, but I felt like I lacked the favor I needed in the situation and my interactions as a whole when all of a sudden feathers began to fall. I am used to seeing feathers periodically, but it was like Jacob's ladder and they were coming down and going back up, but I refused to acknowledge it. I wasn't going to go "Oh!" and get all giddy about it. Finally he asked me, "Are you seeing what I'm seeing?" I said "Yep. It's Jacob's ladder going up and coming down. They're bringing something right now into where we are." He was astounded by it, but I felt very much like "Thank you God" under the circumstances.

I forget how far into the Training for Reigning school we were, but one of the pastors had come to lead worship. I have a blanket that I won't get rid of because it's a dark blue fleece my aunt made me and it is covered with porpoises. I had spread it down on the ground out in the church foyer where there is a small stage at the side. We came into worship and she used her keyboard and I laid down and I just kind of went in the spirit and was praying. I don't want to say I was having visions, but I was praising God and thanking him for the manifestation of those feathers with my pastor, and somehow I got lost in it all. I lost track of time and when worship ended, all of a sudden I heard squeals from one of the girls who was in the class and some other people, and my whole body was outlined with feathers all around me on top of this blanket. This young woman, who I will call Sheila, had never seen any manifestations of the spirit before, so it very much excited her and without me thinking, I asked, "Do you want them." She said "Yes!" so I scraped them all together and gave them to her. Later I felt bad about it because I thought, "Lord, you gave them to me and I guess I should have asked you before I just passed them off, but she was so excited about it."

Everyone knew there weren't usually any feathers around there, and there were like seventeen people present. That next morning the senior pastor led our time of prayer and when we prayed, we'd gather all in a circle and said out whatever was on our spirit. Well, sometimes they would guide us and they may have had something specific they wanted us to do but when it was my turn to pray, no matter what I did I was unable to speak—I just couldn't get the words out. I felt something poking at the roof of my mouth up above my front teeth in the gum line. I reached into my mouth and I pulled out this feather that was a good two inches long and curled. Because the pastor was standing right next to me, he saw me pull this feather out of my gums or something. It actually astonished him so much that he went in and called down to Bethel to some other people and told them about this stuff that kept happening, and asked what it meant. The man my pastor spoke to said, "Well, whoever this person is definitely has the word of God and speaks what He wants her to speak out of her mouth. Because that is an anointed thing."

Cynthia Palmatier

****

Two days ago, I was with a small group of people and we were worshipping to some popular songs that were just being played through a small speaker via someone's iPhone. I was singing in the Spirit and harmonizing with the songs. Afterwards someone told me they saw a lot of angels coming in to the room because of it. After we sat down for discussion there were tiny feathers falling all around the room. This is the third time I have been told angels come in response to my singing, but the first time feathers fell, or at least that I've been aware of.

Diane Pfeiffer-Estep

****

Once I was sitting at my table reading a book by John Crowder and feeling God's presence very strongly. A tiny little white feather landed on the page. I had only recently heard about feathers manifesting, so I thought "huh" and put it in a little wooden box in my room, not sure if I was reading more into in than I should. Several months later, I rather randomly asked an acquaintance to come by so I could pray for his injured foot. Glory spontaneously broke out, and he and I laid hands on my husband and my husband spoke in tongues for the first time. Our friend was so "drunk" on the glory and it was getting so late that I told him he could crash in our spare room and walked him back to show him where it was. Still "drunk" on the glory, he walked into the bedroom, went directly and picked up the little wooden box from on the dresser, opened it and said "Oh look, there's something in here! Here, I'll eat it for you", took out my tiny little feather (that I had never told anyone about) and popped it in his mouth. I stood watching rather stupefied and never even told him until months later!! He said he thought it was lint!!

Gessell Frisbee

****

I drove to JC Penney to look at sweaters. As I walked into the women's section a large, black fluffy feather lay at my feet. It had been a very difficult day but suddenly I felt encouraged by this beautiful gift. In my home, I've had small white feathers drift by me, too. I love my "treasures from God!"

Eva Jean Michelsen

****

Wednesday was such an incredible, humbling, powerful day. Angels had let me and others know they were with us, serving us, showing us that we were not alone; we are a team. At work I noticed a feather but laughed it off as it was behind a door in the dust so I didn't think it was dropped for me (angels drop feathers or dimes around me fairly often now). I turned back around and there were six feathers scattered on the clean floor I had crossed moments ago. Laughing (snorting, actually), I said, "Ok, you guys want something to do," so I prayed and sent the angels to minister to those people who came up in my heart. I turned around to exit the room and three more feathers had appeared on the floor where I had stood looking at the first feather—that's ten white feathers in total and all were different. So here's the best part, I'm in a group that prays for others and no one in the group knew this happened. One of them laid hands on me and as she prayed, she felt the presence of angels and began to sharing about their various functions, so of course I shared about the feathers. All present were encouraged and felt validated by God for He has mandated that we serve His Beloved, His people. Thank you God for giving us a sign and wonder so we would realize how important each of the people we minister to are to You Father God. We are not alone, we are part of a team. We honour You Father God, Jesus and Holy Spirit for all You do in and through us. It is such an incredible honour and privilege to witness the freedom, healing, and empowerment of every soul You bring us to minister to. Thank You for this day!!! I am amazed and astounded, very humbled, and living the dream!!!!

Jen Blunderfield

****

Three of us decided to pray and worship for a season in our old church building. We were free and abandoned to Holy Spirit's leading and we had some beautiful, intimate times of worship and prayer together. Sometimes others joined us too. In the corner of the church we set up a "prayer zone" with cushions and reflective prayer stations. It was in this prayer zone that our first feather appeared.

My friend and I both clearly saw this small feather materialize out of thin air before our eyes. One minute there was empty space. The next minute a feather was floating to the ground in our line of vision. Then another feather appeared on my friend's keyboard as she was preparing to play and worship. After that we had a season of finding feathers in unusual places. I'm not sure that all of them were supernatural. Maybe some were everyday feathers that God placed strategically for us to find, like the pure white one that I found clinging to a peg on the washing line. I can't be certain that particular one materialized out of thin air, but it's pretty odd the way it was perched there on the peg right where I could find it and it made me smile in joy. Another feather showed up in the church where I was to be married a couple of days before my wedding.

There seems to be no particular reason for these feathers that I can think of, except that they cause me to stop and sense Father smiling on us with delight. They bring me into a place of childlike wonder and joy at God's goodness.

Jane

****

A couple months ago when Michael had a social media thread going about gems right as he was releasing the book about gems, I was talking on there. Talking about the manifestations just brought to remembrance all that the Lord had done and as I was meditating on God's goodness, I got up to go to the bathroom, and laying on the carpet inside the bathroom was this huge brown and white feather!

Josh Murphy

****

My husband was in the ICU after having a heart attack and then having a quad by-pass surgery. If the 1st attack hadn't killed him, the "widow maker" would have, the doctor said. He had a word about six years earlier from a prophet that he would not die from a heart attack, like his family members had. I found the feather in his room before the surgery (there were a few days between the heart attack and surgery). God provided the best doctors in cardiac surgery, in the region, the best staff and care. He recovered quite quickly, was released early. God's peace was felt the entire time. It wasn't until after the surgery I was reminded of the word the prophet gave him. Praise God!

Another time, we were attending Grace Center in Franklin, Tennessee, and during worship a feather appeared midair and floated down into the assembly.

Kelly Burris

****

About two years ago I was working at home doing transcription and had been taking a break so I headed to the kitchen to get something to eat. As I walked in the room there was a 2-3" feather on the floor in the doorway. I had walked through that room not long before and it was not there then. I was just very encouraged that the Lord is with me and for me, and the dreams that he's put in my heart were coming to pass.

Misty Chladek

****

It was when we were heading up to Seattle for a conference in 2015, and I look at the dashboard and it was just covered in a bunch of really miniscule, tiny feathers. My friend Hope is like "Sorry, I didn't dust." I was like, "No! You can't dust these! They're angel feathers!" I also have to say that I am waiting for the day that I walk into my room and find a single large feather that covers my entire bed!

Megan Pierce

****

The best experience I have had with God's favor and intimacy when I found these certain feathers, I found two that were purple. They were both different but so incredibly beautiful. We had a house fire so we were staying in the fifth wheel for a while. We had three boys and a dog with us in this fifth wheel and we had to rent a place because my dad needed to rent a place with a trailer hookup. It's a small town so I don't need my credit run thirty-five times. I tried really hard and strived but I found nothing. One day nobody was in the fifth wheel and I had that place clean—I had to because so many people were in it.

I don't own any fluffy things—nothing glittery or anything. I was sitting on the bed and God's presence was so strong on me, I just sobbed with my head in my arms. I cried to God and I felt at peace and at rest, like it just didn't matter even though they were wanting us to leave because of the dog and my son's loud car and everything. It's crunch time. After I had that moment on the bed, I got up and walked out of the small fifth wheel and there outside on the ground was a purple feather. I've never gotten a purple feather before. It was just me alone, and I have had a few ones come, but it was so awesome. Then, I went and walked a little bit further down the steps and there was another one but this was fluffy and the first one was skinny. I still have them in a special box and they're probably three inches long each. It was a beautiful moment and I just know that for the rest of my life that we're not meant to strive but just release it all to God and take the steps in joy because the joy of the Lord is our strength and we can watch him work.

And guess what happened? My son's dad and my boy Dustin were driving around town and this lady was out watering her lawn and she had a sign that she was about to take down because she was going to go to the rental office. They stopped and asked her "Is your house for sale?" It had the RV pad we needed, and it was perfect, complete with three bedrooms. They come back to the trailer and they say "We think we've found a place. We have to go talk to her." We got it. She didn't even run my credit. I had to press in on that a little bit—there was some resistance, but I just talked to her honestly about everything, but she finally just said, "You know what, you can just have it." That's what happens when you give it to Him.

Heather Dawn

****

My first angelic encounter was when I was at a glory meeting, and I felt a huge gust of wind in front of me and I discerned it as an angel. It was awesome, but I didn't pay much attention to it. My second encounter was when I was reading a Smith Wigglesworth book and he was talking about how Jesus uses our hands and feet and I felt two hands around my hands and my face and there was a wind. My angels were touching my body as I was reading. My third encounter was more severe. I was in a class, my teacher was atheist and my faith was always tested. I was the only one who stood up for my faith, also being the only Christian in the class. I asked God to send an angel to comfort me in the next class and He did. That angel hung out with me for the rest of the year in that class

Now here goes to my first angel feather. I was in the living room with a sister in Christ and she said she saw an angel so tall it was going through the ceiling and it had a gold shield and a silver sword. She told me her ear was deaf so I commanded her ear to open and she was healed. Right after I turned around and an angel feather appeared on the air mattress and when I held it my hand was burning with fire. Nights later I was on the phone and lots of angels were in my room and I packed some clothes before heading out for the weekend. That same night I pulled a pair of pants out of my back-pack and a small white feather was stuck on the pants, and again my hand was burning with fire.

Weeks ago I was worshipping in my friend's room and there was wind of multiple angels flying around the room. My friend's siblings came down and they could see the angels flying back and forth through the walls and an angel laid hands on the younger brother while I was praying for him. Days after that I was praying for my sister and she could see angels flying around her. I always have encounters with angels everywhere. My most recent angel feather appeared near my feet while I was in deep worship. Lots of glory!

Zoltan Marossy

****

From February to March 2016 we have been preparing for revival in Los Angeles during that time we held weekly prayer meetings on the last meeting in the beginning of April we had a manna manifestation with an angel feather next to it. We did not fully understand what was going on but kept pressing into the lord. Then on April 26, 2016 we had 80 angel feathers manifest in our bedroom over a three hour period of time. From that point on for 25 days we had angel feathers manifesting throughout the house. We felt the angelic realm was being opened up to us and it was a sign that revival was coming.

Vincent and Sheelah Zavala

****

I have always pondered the meaning of the feathers in response to prayer. I had felt peace many times when the feathers appeared because they represented "God with me" in the midst of the difficulties I was going through. I liked how I hear you put it once,". . . the feather was showing a level of warfare that was happening over this issue." I think that fits my own situation as well.

Once, as I drove to church, I was praying and a feather floated down before my face. I thought, "An angel? Should I move my bag off the passenger's seat?" But I saw no one; just the feather, so I tucked it into my Bible. Walking into church I felt a nudge to check and see if my prayer was answered. I doubted but looked anyway and found that it had been. I have been pondering the idea that the size of feather could be related to size of warfare or the number of people praying. Hence a large congregation praying would get bigger feathers. Mine have always been fairly small, but then I have never gotten them with others, only privately while by myself. I never thought anyone would believe me, so they were my private "pearls". The little tiny feather, that one day, I just figured it was so tiny because it was "little warfare". Yet, I take pleasure in the manifestations no matter the size because it reminds me I am surrounded by God who manifests His interventions in my life.

Rachel Irene Ciardi

****

These are just a few of a multitude of encounters worldwide where people experienced God making feathers appear. The reactions cover a range of emotions from being exited to perplexed to joyful to concerned, but regardless of the response, God is releasing His glory into the earth. In the following chapter we will take a look at what you, the reader, can do to start to experience this miracle in your own life.

Chapter 6

How Do I Get This To Happen?

I never knew that angel feathers were something you could see. I had no idea that we could actually ask for one! I was at a friend's house having my hair done. Her ex-mother-in-law came over and I was introduced to Bev. She was a powerful woman of God and we hit it off right away. We started to talk about the Kingdom and our love for Daddy God. We were laughing and sharing stories when out of the blue she told me that she asked for an angel feather! "Hold it! What did you just say"? I belted out with shock and intrigue, "Is that really possible?" Bev giggled and said, "Oh yes I get them all the time"! She just acted so nonchalant about the whole thing. Inside my mind was freaking out: God doesn't really give people feathers! That's just crazy talk! My hair was finished and we said our goodbyes. As I left the house something inside me was stirred up. I thought ok Daddy if this is real, then I want an angel feather too! I knew that He loves us all equally so if He gave them to Bev then He would give them to me!

I was now on a quest! I was on the lookout for angel feathers. At the time I had birds so looking in my house was a bit challenging. Feathers frequently found their way out of the cage onto the floor. This was going to be hard to distinguish what wasn't from a bird and what from my birds. After prayer I asked Daddy to bring the feathers to my attention. I guess I was still struggling with this being a reality. The wonderful thing about asking Daddy for bringing things to your attention is He will!

One day while at work I was having a conversation at my cosmetic counter, discussing the goodness of God and how faithful He is! As I was speaking something caught my eye, a tiny white feather floating in the air. I looked around to see if maybe someone was cleaning and that dust was being released into the air. No one was around, so I shrugged it off as well that was weird! Now I understand, but back then I thought angel feathers were going to be big! Big Angels meant big feathers. Those teeny tiny feathers had to come from a down coat! I went about my business still looking for angel feathers.

This went on for months. Something would draw my attention to the tiny floating feather. It usually happened when I was be at the counter sharing God stories or prophesying. One hot summer day I was at the counter when out of the corner of my eye I saw a tiny feather. I was looking around for a jacket, but this time it suddenly dawned on me that there are no jackets right now. That's when I got it! They were all angel feathers!! I got super excited and started to then see them all over. Now I spot them and just smile. It's my reminder that angels are around me!

Just recently I was cleaning out my pocketbook when I found a feather inside a pocket! I love that Our Daddy loves to surprise and delight His kids!!

Lisa Perna

****

For those of us who value and enjoy this manifestation but have not personally encountered it, or for whom it does not occur regularly, we may want to know how to start having or increasing the supernatural manifestations we experience. After all, we are blessed when others are blessed, but deep down we all want to experience and perform miracles ourselves. While I wish there was a simple answer and a quick fix that would make it happen, there isn't one, and I haven't been able to make them appear for myself, much less anyone else. In spite of not having all the answers, I do believe we can position ourselves to receive from heaven both to encounter this miracle and see it increase in our lives. Miracles operates on fixed principles, much like a very complicated math equation, and while we as the Church don't know all of the variables to solve for x (which in this case x=feathers), we have figured out some of them. I will do my best to explain here what a person can do to partner with heaven to see these types of things come to pass.

The first key is to engage angels. While to some, as we mentioned in a previous chapter, the fear of angel worship comes up, but this isn't what we are doing. We are co-laborers in this world and work together. I don't worship my coworkers, but I do respect them and appreciate the help they provide me in my nursing career. I attempt to provide them with assistance as well—it's a give and take relationship and angels are the same. How do we help angels? John Mulinde, an apostle in Africa, writes of a conversation he had with a former warlock in his essay "Combat in The Heavenly Realms:

How Satan Stops our Prayers." Mulinde outlines the
following in his conversation with the warlock:

> Then he said something that was difficult to receive:
> If the one who prays knows of the spiritual armor and
> is clothed with it, the answer comes by an angel who is
> also clothed in full armor.

> However, if the one who prays doesn't care about
> being clothed in spiritual armor, their angel comes to
> them without spiritual armor. When Christians are
> careless about the kinds of thoughts that enter their
> minds and do not fight the battle for their minds, their
> angels come to them without helmets. Whatever
> spiritual weapon you ignore on earth, your angel does
> not have it when he serves you. In other words, our
> spiritual armor is not protecting our physical bodies; it
> is protecting our spiritual exploits.

> The man said that as the angel was coming they
> would watch him to find the areas that were uncovered,
> and then attack those areas. If he didn't have a helmet,
> they would shoot at his head. If he didn't have a
> breastplate, they would shoot at his chest. If he didn't
> have shoes, they would make a fire, causing him to
> have to walk through fire.

Angels are people too. Well, not in the way we typically
consider, but angels are like humans in that they have feelings
and thoughts and seem to be able to experience sensations.
They are not spiritual robots, but possess intellect, reason, and

will, much like us. They enjoy being around followers of Jesus who are filled with His light and who emanate His glory.

I once read something a friend wrote who said that angels on assignment from heaven can actually heal when they are in the presence of believers who are worshiping, so if we are under spiritual attack it is important we spend time in worship to help prepare our angels for combat. The reason I share all this is to show that angels are beings we can actively partner with to see God's glory realm manifest and to give permission to those who are still on the fence about the idea. Additionally, considering I mentioned in Chapter 2 that feathers may appear when angels are spiritually battling over us, it seems reasonable to me that we might also see feathers appear when angels are healing up during our times of worship. A related point to note is that because angels are attracted to worship, while regular worship will not force feathers to appear, it will increase the angelic presence in your home or gathering, which can only help.

I believe we can also ask God to specifically assign one or more angels to us to bring this manifestation. In Matthew 26:53, Jesus spoke to Satan about this saying, "Do you think I cannot call on my Father, and he will at once put at my disposal more than twelve legions of angels?" Jesus knew that while twelve legions of angels were not at his disposal at that very moment, they were but a single prayer away. As Jesus modeled this, I believe we too can ask the Father to put angels at our disposal to bring this manifestation to us, and I have asked him on multiple occasions. There doesn't need to be some deep, drawn out and lengthy prayer to accomplish this; a simple request will do. God wants to give us these feather experiences and oftentimes we don't receive things because we don't ask for them (James 4:2b)! Jesus states the converse of this quite plain in Matthew 7:7-8 which says, "Ask and it shall be given to you; seek and you shall find; knock and the door shall be opened. For everyone who asks, receives; he who seeks, finds; and to him to knocks, the door shall be opened."

Jesus spoke of this matter, "Do not be afraid, little flock, for your Father has been pleased to give you the kingdom" (Luke 12:32). If it gives God pleasure to give us gifts, then we might as well ask Him for them since He has already told us to! In this passage, Jesus was encouraging his disciples not to worry about things either as worrying doesn't help change reality in fruitful ways. Rather, it may hinder the blessings God wants to bring because many things in the Kingdom occur, at least in part according to our faith and worry counteracts faith.

This brings us to our next key, which is two-fold: engage and increase faith, and decrease and disengage from worry and doubt. Doubt and worry go hand in hand because worry is usually our mind entertaining the reality that we will be disappointed with what we experience. In other words, worry is what happens when we let our doubts control our thoughts. If we doubt that God will manifest something and start to dwell on our concern, it is worry and feeds all the wrong things. On the other hand, when we focus our minds on

God's plans, we will engage our faith and let it produce a harvest of righteousness in our lives.

There is an old Cherokee tale about a grandfather teaching his grandson about life, and he told the boy a story about two wolves fighting — one who is good and kind and only fights when attacked and who always seeks the best in everyone. The second wolf is angry and mean and evil and fights everyone all the time. He is angry for no reason and will attack without provocation. As the story goes, the grandfather explained that these wolves are alive inside of him fighting every day. "Who wins?" the young boy asks? The grandfather answered, "The one I feed." I believe this story is a good representation of the tension between faith and doubt.

A while back I had God nudge me subtly at work about my thoughts and how I did and did not engage faith. I began asking the question "Will this happen?" before I was praying for healing for my patients. The problem is that when we start by asking that question, we really destroy any outlet that faith might have to take root and express itself because when we entertain the possibility that the answer is "No, it will not happen," that's it—faith is gone. Instead, we might ask another questions, "Does God want me to experience this?" In addition to being a better question, the answer is a resounding "Yes!" As I mentioned a few paragraphs earlier, God takes great joy in giving us the Kingdom of God—after all, Psalm 16:11 says, "You make known to me the path of life; you will fill me with joy in your presence, with eternal pleasures at your right hand." God is seriously interested in us experiencing His joy and pleasure. Not only that, but we must not forget that when God first created humans he placed them in a garden full of wonderful delights in a land by the name of Pleasure--because that's what Eden means!

There are many things in life we cannot control, and while I cannot make other people have faith for things nor can I always perfect the spiritual atmosphere of a room or a region, I am able to make choices that help me cultivate a lifestyle of faith. In other words, it doesn't matter what else is happening around me. Faith is not simply obtained; it is grown. Jesus told many parables, but when he spoke of faith, he compared it to a mustard seed—something that grows and produces more fruit than anything else in the garden. Faith may not start out looking like much, but much like the wolf in the story, it will grow big and strong if we feed it properly.

One night in 2015 I was at a meeting in Albany, Oregon with a precious group of believers who were hungry for God and gathered regularly to seek Him and to engage the supernatural realms. This particular meeting was set aside to seek the Lord in faith and expectation for gemstones from heaven to manifest. Many of those at the meeting had experienced this before, but there were those there who had not yet but wanted to. I was invited by a friend, and although my wife and I did not attend as guest speakers by any means, we were invited to share a few words about the gem manifestation.

I spoke for about five minutes and after sharing a brief testimony, I encouraged everyone present that God wanted to give them gems—personally. God loves each and every one of us and desires to directly interact with each of us. He desires to lavish gifts on each one, and we are not so special that God won't do for us what he does for many others, whether it be gems or any other miracle. I encouraged the group to actually go around the room and look for gems as God is a good Father and loves to give his kids gifts that they'll enjoy, much like any earthly parent gives their children fun toys to play with just to see their enjoyment. I let them know that looking for gems isn't a sign of valuing gems over God, but that we are simply getting to appreciate the gifts that God is giving us—we're not seeking His hands *instead* of His face, but we want to both know God *and* get the goodies!

No sooner had I shared this than a well-meaning but misguided woman did the favor of sharing a short testimony with exhortation that we were definitely *not* to look for gems at any moment whatsoever, and that we were to worship the Lord only and not get off into idolatry with this gem-business. If God wants us to have gems, He knows where to put them so we will find them without searching for them. I must confess, I was *very* disappointed to hear this. This woman, and the demons within her that spurred on such interaction, singlehandedly dealt a huge blow to the growing faith in the room, and I am sorry to say that I don't think it ever quite recovered.

I am sure if I had been prone to arguing, we could have gotten into one as this woman had a very contrary attitude. I was gracious with her disagreement, even backpedaling slightly in stating that each person needed to decide what was in his her or her heart with the Lord in how to address this issue she had brought up. In reality the woman was dead-wrong and I probably should have said as much for the sake of everyone else present. She was determined to pursue the issue and made sure she had the last word on the subject so that everyone would bow to her will on the matter. How can I say she was wrong? In Matthew 7: 7-8 it says, "Ask and it will be given to you; seek and you will find; knock and the door will be opened to you. For everyone who asks receives; the one who seeks finds; and to the one who knocks, the door will be opened." Jesus directly instructed his disciples to ask and seek, and if Jesus says it, we should probably do it.

A short while later during worship, the Lord instructed me to get up and start looking for gems, telling me that if I didn't, they definitely would not appear. I realized that this woman's words had put everyone in a state where they didn't want to offend her and weren't going to look for gems. I got up and walked across the middle of the room and began searching on the far side of the room from her. After I did so, a couple other people got up and started to do the same. It wasn't too long after that this woman left the meeting, and after she was gone even more people began to search in earnest, and the gathering took a much lighter, more enjoyable tone.

Although no gems appeared that night, there was one supernatural occurrence that evening. While the woman was still present, I found a single small white feather near me on the floor. While everyone there was praying and believing for gems, I am pretty familiar with feathers, having experienced them over the years at home, church, at my workplace, and even in random public places. In this case, I believe its appearance showed a level of warfare that was happening over this issue of supernatural manifestations. I was pleased the feather appeared, but I was disappointed it didn't progress any further and no gems appeared afterward.

This meeting was a bit of an object lesson for me in regards to things-supernatural. We often do not realize the power of our words and the attitude and intention behind those words. We have the ability to create and encourage faith as my wife and I had done with the things we shared, and we have the power to sow doubt as that woman had done. I wish I could give her the benefit of the doubt and say that she did it unwittingly, but the purpose of the meeting was no secret, and if she didn't want to be around people who were looking for gems, it would have been better for all of us if she had chosen not to attend.

Faith is a tenuous thing at times, and when faith is wavering or new, the smallest things can tip it one way or the other. It is important, therefore, that we encourage and cultivate lifestyles of faith that push us toward heavenly realities on a daily basis. A single feather from heaven was all that appeared out of a group of around thirty believers, many of whom have already seen and a few of whom currently still experience this on occasion in their own homes, and all of whom had been praying that week and that day for angels to bring gemstones into the meeting. That feather served as a bit of a lesson to me—that not only do I have a lot to learn about dealing with contrary people in large group meetings, but that more important than just those people are the influence they have on the rest of the people present.

There really isn't much to avoiding doubt except by developing habits to switch our thinking to something else when we start to doubt and worry. This stops the thought cycle that, if given long enough, will derail things. In the above story, the woman was very successful in derailing the faith of those present by putting their thoughts on things they didn't need to focus on, and while I believe she was also unwittingly a tool of the enemy in that moment, she had a responsibility to those around her to work to not destroy their faith. While Paul was addressing a slightly different concept, the following passage can be correlated with what I believe our responsibility is toward others in regards to helping build faith instead of sowing doubt.

> Be careful, however, that the exercise of your rights does not become a stumbling block to the weak. For if someone with a weak conscience sees you, with all your knowledge, eating in an idol's temple, won't that person be emboldened to eat what is sacrificed to idols? So this weak brother or sister, for whom Christ died, is destroyed by your knowledge. When you sin against them in this way and wound their weak conscience, you sin against Christ. Therefore, if what I eat causes my brother or sister to fall into sin, I will never eat meat

again, so that I will not cause them to fall. (1
Corinthians 8:9-13)

All of 1 Corinthians 8 addresses this subject of eating food
sacrificed to idols and how our faith can affect someone else
and is worth going back and reading, but I want to explore this
concept a little further.

We are not inherently wrong if we believe differently than
others on a subject as that woman in the meeting did about
searching for gems. It's perfectly fine that she felt God show
her not to look; it would have been going against her own
conscience if she had started looking—and I wouldn't want
her to do that. On the other hand, as the passage above
shows us, we need to watch to make sure that exercising our
own faith doesn't destroy someone else's. When the woman
shared a testimony and spoke a message that counteracted the
faith we were building in everyone present, she didn't cause
anyone to sin, but she was a stumbling block and true to form,
the results of sowing that doubt and becoming that stumbling
block were obvious. It shifted me and I am very accustomed
to these manifestations—how could it not have worked
against everyone else's faith as well? We must be conscious
that we use our words wisely to build faith and tear down
doubt instead of the other way around.

In the first book in this series, "Gemstones from Heaven,"
I gave an illustration about how miracles work and why one
person might experience something and another might not.

Imagine a group of children all gathered around a gumball machine, and all of them are drooling over the multicolored gumballs before them. One girl steps forward, pulls a quarter out of her pocket, pops it in the machine, and turns the knob. Like clockwork, the levers turn and a gumball drops into the slot below, which the child promptly puts in her mouth and the corners of her lips turn up into a smile. Some of the other children look at her with disappointment, wishing they, too could have a gumball. One boy turns and runs away, only to return a minute later with a quarter as well and he, too, is rewarded with a gumball. Soon, some of the children scatter, returning with quarters as well, while some other children continue to stare disappointedly at the heartless machine that refuses to give them candy. A bit later someone else walks up with a stack of quarters and starts popping gumballs from the machine and handing them out left and right until a number of children who didn't have quarters of their own also get some candy.

Miracles, for all their unpredictability, do have a few predictable components. Much like putting a quarter in a machine, if you have the right currency, you can access miracles at any time. In this illustration then, God is like the gumball machine. He isn't partial about who gets to receive miracles or healing or anything else, but if the proper currency isn't present, it simply isn't going to happen. The first child used faith, the currency of heaven, to access the treasure. The second child, and those thereafter, didn't have the necessary faith, but they went out and got some and returned with fruit for their labors. The final child was someone who carried enough currency that it didn't matter if another child had any or not—theirs was sufficient for a number of people to access the treasure. In dealing with disappointment, it is partially not completely, a faith problem. If we, too, had faith, we would see more gems than we do now. While this can sound insulting to some, it's not meant that way at all. Rather, if low faith really is a problem, then much like a medical diagnosis, it can be hard to treat a problem until you know what it is. If low faith is your problem, then you can now do something about it! Don't be like the children who stare at the machine hoping they can have one, but look at how you can go out and get the faith you need for the manifestation (King).

It can be easy when hearing someone talk about faith to turn off your listening ears and glaze over the words. This happens to me sometimes, but I believe that it is partly because there is so little practical teaching on the subject. Hebrews 11:1 says, "Now faith is the substance of things hoped for, the evidence of things not seen" (*NKJV*). Think of a periodic table—all of the elements listed there have their own characteristics such as weight, density, and other properties such as durability, heat conduction, etc. Faith is an actual thing—a spiritual element with the property of creation. It is the spiritual building block to all of reality, and when we engage it we release a literal substance into the atmosphere! God used this same creative power of faith when He spoke the heavens and the earth into existence. If it is powerful enough to create the universe, then when we use it we can also can see miracles happen! If this is an area of weakness for you, I encourage you to find ways to increase your faith and see what God opens up before you!"

This brings us to the third key to this manifestation—the power of the tongue. When we speak the will of God, we change reality around us. When we speak against the will of God, we also change reality, but not in ways that bring life. After all, Proverbs 18:21 says, "The tongue has the power of life and death, and those who love it will eat its fruit." Regardless of what and how we speak, we will get results based on our declaration. Remember that Jesus once healed two blind men and said to them, "According to your faith let it be done to you" (Matthew 9:29b). In Luke 17:19 Jesus healed ten lepers, and said to the one who returned, "Rise and go; your faith has made you well." Another time a woman grabbed his clothing and he felt power flow out of him: "Jesus turned and saw her. 'Take heart, daughter,' he said, 'your faith has healed you.' And the woman was healed at that moment" (Matthew 9:22). Jesus declared that their faith—often demonstrated by the words they spoke, made them well. When we speak out life, we receive it back because it makes a mockery of God to think that we can sow and not reap (Galatians 6:7). Declaration, then, is one of the ways we can experience this feather-miracle. Declare it in your life!

Declare it in your home! Decree that you live a life of miracles! At the end of this book I have included a prayer—my prayer for you to experience this manifestation. I encourage you to read it out loud and declare it over your life; I have also read it out loud and prayed it over everyone who reads this book.

The fourth key to see this manifestation occur is the gift of miracles. What makes feathers appear around some people on a massive scale when others only see a feather or two on rare occasion, or for others they have yet to experience this heavenly grace. I believe that one logical reason behind this is that some, whether they know it or not, operate in a gift of miracles for feathers appearing. When one operates in a gift, there is more of a direct pipeline from heaven in regards to that particular miracle. Thus, what might be extremely infrequent for one person who doesn't have a gift will be a regular occurrence for someone who operates in that particular grace. Different people have the gift operating at different strengths and in different ways, so things such as how frequent feathers show up or how unique the feathers are that appear will differ from person to person.

I firmly believe that we can impart spiritual gifts from person to person. In reality when we receive the Holy Spirit, we don't receive part of his arm while someone else gets His leg and another person his left ear only—we all receive the same Spirit that the Bible says He gives to ALL as He wills it (1 Corinthians 12:11). In other words, Holy Spirit isn't holding back from us because He wills and desires to give *all* of the spiritual gifts to each of us. Paul mentioned in 1

Timothy 4:14 and again in 2 Timothy 1:6 that the elders of Timothy's church had imparted a spiritual gift to him when they laid hands on him. If we want to see more miracles, and specifically feathers, we should get those who operate in these supernatural graces to lay hands on us and pray that we receive the gift of miracles and for the feathers to appear to us. When we do this, we should not be surprised if the gift comes to us, and we should also not be surprised if the manifestation does not occur with the same frequency, size, or any other defining characteristic in the same manner as the one who prayed for us. I firmly believe that when someone prays for me to receive a spiritual gift that I have indeed received it, but typically these things come in what I refer to as "seed form."

Imagine that each person has a "Spiritual Gift Garden" where each spiritual gift is represented by a plant. Because the Spirit is given without limit, each garden will have one of every plant in existence, but the size and shape of each plant will vary. If it's the same Spirit and the same skills, then why would the plants look different from garden to garden? First Corinthians 12:4-6 says, "There are different kinds of gifts, but the same Spirit distributes them. There are different kinds of service, but the same Lord. There are different kinds of working, but in all of them and in everyone it is the same God at work." Even though all the gifts themselves are given by the same Spirit, they work differently from person to person. This could be compared to the difference in plant shape in the above analogy. An example of this is two people who operate in the gift of prophecy but one only ever has visions and the other never has visions but hears God's voice speaking inside his head. Both will be able to prophesy, but the way that gift operates is a bit different.

Plant size, however, has to do with the level of the gift. When I refer to spiritual gifts as having levels, I am referring to the idea that as with all things in life, skills and spiritual gifts both go through stages of growth. It is utterly rare and verging on impossible to find someone who can play a musical instrument like a master musician from day one, and there are varying skill levels along the journey to become a master. A low-level spiritual gift, which is one that is simply not well-developed yet, could be compared to a baby plant that is maybe only an inch or two tall, whereas a high level gift would be better represented by a full-grown fruit-bearing plant. 1 Corinthians 12:11 states, "All these are the work of one and the same Spirit, and He distributes them to each one, just as he determines." The "distributes to each one, just as He determines" doesn't mean we don't have the ability to access certain gifts but that Holy Spirit decides whether someone's spiritual gift starts at a beginner level, intermediate, or possibly even a higher level. Still, all spiritual gifts can be grown and increased through use and over time.

What does this look like? When we receive a seed, it has the potential to grow into a mature plant, but until that seed is planted and watered, nothing will happen. Likewise, when someone lays hands on us and prays for us to receive a gift, it is the same as them handing us a seed. What we do with that seed over time makes all the difference in the world. Mentally putting that seed on a shelf and failing to practice and develop it will yield no results—essentially crop failure. On the other hand, if we tend that spiritual gift by activating our faith, through prayer, declaration, and practice, and so long as we weed out the doubt, the seed should flourish and bear good fruit.

While having hands laid on us is good, there is another way we can engage this feather manifestation—and really, most anything in the Kingdom. Oftentimes proximity can have as much of an effect on whether we receive a spiritual gift as anything else. There is something about being around someone with the feather manifestation, or any other gift for that matter, that being in their presence tends to accelerate the "plant growth" in our own life. The best explanation I can give is a musical one, where when two similar notes are played on two strings, the vibrations they each give off will influence the other vibrating string. Often, the strings will do what is called entrainment, where one string will cause the second string to change the speed it vibrates at to match the first. In other words, the first string causes the second string to change because of an invisible, intangible quality—yet tangible or not, the pitch changes. There appears to be something about Kingdom experiences that cause a form of spiritual resonance to entrain us into these types of manifestations as we spend time around others already walking in it. Regardless of how one understands this phenomenon, just be aware that spending time with others with a gift may cause us to walk in it. Honoring one another is a good way to help release this as the Bible tells us that when we honor one another for who they are and what they walk in, we can receive a reward that matches how we honor them (Matthew 10:41).

The next and related key is that of engaging spiritual atmospheres. Sometimes when we are in the presence of other people, something about their life journey and the experiences they have had create an opening in the spirit for us to encounter similar things. The way I describe it is that their life experiences take on a tangible spiritual quality and alter the atmosphere around them, much like an invisible energy field around their body. Whether we can see it or not, the force field is there making things easier for us to enter in. I have shared this in other books, but I have two friends who are both very prophetic, but my friend Beth has stated on numerous occasions that when hanging around our other friend Hope that she always gets revelation more frequently. Although she would never say it to anyone else, Hope is a prophet. Being in Hope's presence brings increased revelation because there is something about the Holy Spirit working in and through Hope that further enhances Beth's strong prophetic gifts—and the same can happen to others as well! I find that when I am around other prophetic people that spontaneous worship flows more easily for me. I am fairly prophetic already, but at times the words come to me more easily or the tune is simpler to follow than others. I have had times when singing with a few others that we all clicked really well, and while the lyrics we sang were entirely improvised on the spot without discussing with one another, we all devised lyrics that matched perfectly. This is the sort of effect we can expect when there is a heavenly atmosphere, usually carried by those present, that brings everyone to a higher level of experience. When we get around others with the feather manifestation, the likelihood of engaging that realm in our lives increases.

The next key is to pray and ask God for revelation on how to engage the feather miracle. The keys I have shared thus far can be useful, but there is no substitute for a now-word from God telling us what He is doing in our lives. If we aren't experiencing feathers, maybe God has some suggestions for us. Maybe there are things such as unforgiveness and dishonor in our lives that are allowing the enemy to block what God wants to do. God may have other things He wants to share with us as well, and the only way we will discover those things is if we take some time to chat with Him about it although we must be sure to let Him do most of the chatting. Maybe God wants to share something to build our faith. Maybe He has some exercises He wants us to do to help move us into a place where we are able to receive. Maybe God isn't giving us feathers right now because it would be a distraction from what He wants to do with us in this moment. I know that in the past when I have prayed about gems and feathers appearing with more frequency, God has gently nudged me that He wants to give them to me, but that He doesn't want me to focus on a single miracle manifestation, but many. There are times where if God were to give me tons of feathers it would shift my focus in unhelpful ways. That doesn't mean God will never do it, but my timing might not match up with His, and in those situations I need to be patient.

When the "No" is really a "Not right now," it is easy to get frustrated. I try not to whine to God, as complaining is unattractive, but there are certainly times where I wish God would speed the process up by about a billion times. Did I mention that I am generally impatient? I believe that Jesus paid the price for everything already, which in my mind means I should have everything . . . immediately. I expect people to get healed on the spot when I pray for them, and I expect God to manifest His goodness in keeping with my timetable—right away! Nevertheless, God's timing is much more complex, all-encompassing, and perfect. There are usually other factors in play that I don't know about—such as the other forty-six parts of the "miracles now" equation we have been working on in this chapter. The good news is that just because something hasn't happened yet doesn't mean it won't in the future. There is a saying that goes "God is rarely early and never late, but he is always on time." When things aren't happening on our schedules, sometimes we need to release that schedule to God and let God be God and other times we need to change something in our own lives—but we won't know which it is unless we ask God first.

Another key to this manifestation is warfare. A real-live battle is raging all around us in the spiritual spheres over whether God's will is made manifest in the earth or not. As such, I am not a big proponent of the "open door closed door" theory that many Christians follow—where if an opportunity opens then it automatically must be God's blessing and if the door closes, it cannot be anything other than God's protection. While I do ask God to open and close doors, I don't believe we can automatically assume a result is God regardless of the outcome. Those well-meaning people who do believe this often quote from the book of Job saying, "The Lord gives and the Lord takes away, blessed be the name of the Lord." In other words, whatever happens is God's will. The main problem with this, other than the fact that Job had an inferior revelation of God that didn't include the nature of Jesus, is that of the ancient Hebrew mindset. This historic way of looking at the world was one that had no room for the idea that we should do war against evil spirits because they believed God was in charge of everything in the same way that the pendulum of a grandfather clock ultimately controls the whole clock. While the pendulum isn't directly attached to each and every gear in the clock, if the pendulum stops so does the clock.

Tyler Johnson, in his book *How to Raise the Dead* does a wonderful job of explaining the Hebrew mindset about God's sovereignty and authority:

> Hebrews viewed God and His angels in the same way. If God sent an angel, sometimes it is referred to in scripture as the Angel of the Lord, and sometimes it is simply referred to as The Lord. There was no line drawn between the angel and God, because the angel was carrying out God's bidding, acting in His authority, and thus was, in essence, The Lord. This view was an assumed cultural norm in those days, and the scriptures are written in light of it.

The problematic aspect of this is that at one time, satan and his angels were servants of God. They were Angels of the Lord. But long ago they chose to rebel against God and serve their own evil desires. The problem with the Hebraic view is that it didn't fully acknowledge that satan rebelled against God. Instead of recognizing that satan was in total opposition to God and an enemy to God, the Hebrews believed that the enemy was still a tool in the hand of God. Because of their distorted view of God's sovereignty (that many have today), they believed that everything that happened must be God's doing. They concluded that God would make use of satan when He had something distasteful to deal out to humanity like judgments, punishments, wrath, and death. They figured that when Satan did something, it was ultimately God's doing anyways because God was sovereign over all. In reality, the enemy was no longer a messenger of God's will, nor a friend of God, but the Hebraic mindset still encompassed satan's acts as God's. . .

. . . The devil is brought up in the Old Testament very few times compared to in the New Testament. Though very few writers of the Old Testament mention the devil, every writer in the New Testament does. To the Hebrew mind, because satan was seen as a servant of God, there was no reason to bring him up. This changed in the New Testament because Christ came and enlightened humanity of the reality of the devil. In fact, one of Jesus' aims in ministry was to awaken people to the reality that there was an enemy that was bent on their destruction. Jesus said that the very reason He came to Earth was to destroy the works of the devil (1 John 3:18), because man wasn't even aware of the works of the devil. (143-144, 147)

It's easy to see how a belief system like that could influence an entire culture to not understand spiritual warfare. We, on the other hand, cannot afford to live from that kind of mentality as the battle is real and goes on daily in our lives. How does this relate to heavenly feathers and miracles? Angels and demons fight every day over the choices we make and how much influence they get to have on those choices. The image of the conscience sitting on our shoulders with an angel whispering in one ear and a demon whispering in the other ear isn't far off. They fight each other for dominance in our lives, and not because angels intend or want to dominate us, but because they want to prevent the demons from dominating us, and when angels are allowed a greater influence in our lives, we are more peace-filled, loving, kind, and exude more godly qualities as a result of the atmosphere these heavenly beings release toward us.

If we want feathers to manifest in our lives, we may need to engage the battle. If we aren't hitting the miracle breakthrough we seek, it could be that demons are fighting the very angels in the heavens who carry the answers we seek. In the Bible, in the book of Daniel, Chapter 10 tells the story of Daniel's encounter with a heavenly being who was carrying a message to deliver to Daniel directly from God. Daniel had prayed 21 days prior to the messenger arriving, but the messenger was delayed because he had to fight against the Prince of Persia who seemed to have set up a blockade of some kind in the spirit. This messenger took 21 days from the time he left from heaven to fight past this demon prince in order to successfully deliver the message to Daniel. While we may not think of the heavens or the spiritual realm as a whole as having distance and regions much like locations on earth, it does. Different spirits occupy different regions, and many of them do not serve God. When angels pass through bearing messages, spiritual gifts, and answers to prayer, these spirits attempt to waylay them and steal the goods. In "Combat in The Heavenly Realms: How Satan Stops our Prayers" Author John Mulinde explains this dynamic:

> When they overpower an angel of God, the first thing they go after is the answer he is carrying, and they get it from him. They then give it to people who are involved in cults or witchcraft, so people might say, 'I got this because of witchcraft.'

> Remember what the Bible says in the book of James? All good things come from God. So where does the devil get the things he gives to his people? Some people who cannot have children go to witch doctors and satanists and become pregnant! Who gave them the baby? Is satan a creator? No! He steals from those who don't pray through to the end. Jesus said, 'Pray without ceasing' (1 Thessalonians 5:17). And then He said, 'But when the Son of Man comes, will

He find faith?' (Luke 18:8). Will He find you still waiting? Or will you have given up, and the enemy stolen what you prayed for?

Then the man said that they were not satisfied with just stealing the answer. They were also interested in detaining the angel. They would start fighting against him. And he said that sometimes they would succeed in holding and binding the angel. He said that when that happens, the Christian on earth becomes a victim as well. They can do anything to that Christian because he is left totally without ministry in the spiritual realm.

I asked him, 'Do you mean that an angel can be held captive by demonic forces?' . . . He said that they could not hold the angel very long because as other Christians prayed elsewhere, reinforcements would come and the angels would go free. However, if the Christian responsible did not pray through, he remained a captive. Then the enemy would send his own angel to them as an angel of light. That is how deception comes—false visions and false prophecies, false leading or guidance in the spirit, and the making of all kinds of wrong decisions. And many times this person is open to all kinds of attacks and bondages.

We cannot rely on angels to do things without our assistance, because they are also under attack by the enemy. This is not meant to sound fatalistic as though nothing will happen if we don't spend five weeks out of the year in fasting and prayer, and another four hours daily in intercession. What I am pointing out here are the spiritual dynamics with which we need to be aware. Sometimes we pray and things come easily and quickly. Other times there is warfare we have to push through. I believe that signs and wonders come with a significant amount of warfare—or else everyone we know would experience them regularly. As such, if we want to experience supernatural manifestations, we will probably need to spend some time in prayer. It is best to ask the Lord for guidance on what and how to pray, as God has much wisdom He desires to give us and to help us know what and how to pray. After all, maybe there is an angel on his or her way to us right now carrying basketfuls of feathers!

While having the gift of miracles, as mentioned earlier in this chapter, is extremely beneficial, and operating out of faith is likewise useful, they are of far less benefit if we don't understand how things work. One of my observations, which conversations I have had with God and angels have only worked to confirm, is that all of creation could be expressed in numbers. Now I am no mathematician, but all matter is energy, and energy functions through finite, definable, measurable reactions, so it's not too far of a stretch to say that literally all creation functions much like a complex series of math equations. The centrifugal force created by the earth's rotation combined with the gravitational pull exerted on us, along with the weight of the molecules in the atmosphere and the gravity working on them, along with the various other forces in play, decide things such as the flow of the tides and why we are unable to fly. However, what if we were able to overcome those limiting forces? How much energy would that take? And where would that energy come from? In theory, if one had a limitless supply of energy they could put into any form they desire, anything is possible. Incidentally, God has that limitless supply of energy, and as Jesus said in Luke 18:27 (and again in Matthew 19:26 and Mark 10:27), "What is impossible with man is possible with God."

The ability to understand miracles and how they work, I believe has much to do with our ability to understand that everything in creation requires energy of some kind and involves some sort of transaction. Faith is a force that causes things to happen. Why? Because whatever form of energy, whether physical or spiritual, that faith exerts, has the ability to influence and change reality. I believe it's why Paul said, "Now to him who is able to do immeasurably more than all we ask or imagine, according to his power that is at work within us . . ." (Ephesians 3:20). In other words, the power and energy we exert has a definite influence on what and how things do and do not happen. While God is able to do more than we can ask or think, there is something about the power at work within us that makes a significant difference.

While this may seem far-fetched to some, Revelation 5:8 speaks of the prayers of the saints as being collected in golden bowls. Later on, in Revelation 8, the incense made up of prayers is combined with the fire of God then thrown back down onto the earth. In that passage, the end result of the prayers and fire being thrown back to the earth were colossal, earth-shattering changes. While a single prayer might not seem significant, I believe these passages demonstrate the principle I am describing—that there are mathematical, measurable quantities of power, often arrived at through prayer, needed to bring change into the earth. The Bible mentions multiple times that God acted when "times had reached their fullness." Like with the bowls when the necessary amount of time had passed, God moved. When we pray, we have the disadvantage of not knowing when these spiritual bowls have become full, but when they do, the answers we seek are sent to us. When we want to break through into something new, such as feathers appearing from heaven, we may need to pray until that bowl is filled, and only then will we get our answer.

I believe the final key to experience this manifestation is joy. I know I have shared a number of keys that could take a lot of time and effort if someone really went after it wholeheartedly. The problem with this is that when we start to work at things, we can get to a place where instead of engaging with God, we are striving and trying to force God, the angels, and the rest of the universe to bend to our will. And while I do believe God gives us keys such as those found in this chapter to be able to steward and administrate the goings-on of the cosmos, we also need to lighten up and have fun from time to time. It can be easier than we might think to get so focused on getting results that we forget the fun in the feathers—that it can honestly be a complete and total blast when these things appear! And just the idea that God would send us heavenly feathers itself should seem fun. I believe that when it stops getting exciting and seeking the sign has become drudgery, we need to take a break, refill our lives with God's joy, and then connect with God about how to proceed from there. So much of what we do in life can be drudgery—let's not let this miracle become one too.

Before we move on to the next chapter where I share one final testimony to stretch your faith, I want to encourage and remind you that experiencing this feather miracle is something God *wants* for you. God does not withhold good things from His children because He is a good God—so regardless of your circumstances, how worthy you perceive you are or not, or anything else, all of that is irrelevant to the fact that our God is kind, loving, gentle, gracious, looks upon you with favor, and already knows your desire to live this out. So ask, seek, and knock freely knowing that the Father of Heavenly Lights is shining His gaze down upon you with love and excitement for the blessings He has for you.

Chapter 7

Feathers From Heaven

The testimony you are about to read is in a category all on its own. The large feather on the cover image is a photo I took of the one in this story when I was interviewing pastors John and Ruth Filler of Gateway Church in Coeur D'Alene, Idaho. John was the one who shared this story about some encounters he and a parishioner had. What sets this particular testimony apart from the rest is that while we usually think of feathers appearing from heaven, what would it be like if someone went to heaven and got the feather for themselves? Read on and find out as John shares:

It was the spring of 2007 when I preached a message out of Isaiah 40 on the verses about making the way for the Lord:

A voice of one calling: "In the wilderness prepare the way for the Lord; make straight in the desert a highway for our God. Every valley shall be raised up, every mountain and hill made low; the rough ground shall become level, the rugged places a plain. And the glory of the Lord will be revealed, and all people will see it   together. For the mouth of the Lord has spoken.'

I ended the meeting by dividing people into groups and instructed, "By the Spirit I want you to choose one of the four areas you are struggling in, and I want you to gather together and pray for each other in those four different arenas. People started moving into group, and this man named Terry went into the Mountains Made Low group. When he went into that group, he began to talk to people until all of a sudden he was taken by the Spirit into a trance.

The group members said they left him alone because they knew he had gone somewhere in the spirit. When he came out of the trance he was shaking, both physically and emotionally. He shared his experience with his group and after he finished, he came up to where I was standing at the podium and started talking to me about his encounter. I could tell he was rattled. He said that when he entered the group, the Spirit of the Lord came upon him and he was taken into history into the Valley of Dry Bones. He said that he felt like his wife was alongside him in the spirit. He saw a host of angels around the entire valley and a myriad of angels hovering over the valley speaking and singing life over the bones.

He said, 'I was watching this and it was absolutely incredible to see what I was seeing. Then I remembered by the Spirit that you had taught us that any time God takes you to a different dimension to always pick something up and bring it back with you. So I reached down and without looking what it was, I grabbed it and shoved it in my pocket. I haven't even looked to see what it is in my pocket.' He was still shaking.

I {John} said, 'We've had gold dust and we've had manna and gemstones. The worst it could be is a bone.' I was just teasing him a bit, but I then said, 'You need to pull it out of your pocket.' Terry reached into his pocket and pulled the unknown object out and it was this amazing, beautiful, incredible white feather. He was still standing there shaking, as he has always been uncomfortable with this sort of thing, and I had my Bible, the same Bible I still use today, with me held between my left arm and my body. I was ready to walk away after he showed me this feather when all of a sudden he grabbed my Bible, opened it up and shoved it randomly in and said, 'Here, you have it.'

'You're kidding me! You just brought something back that you just got from another dimension and you're giving it to me?'

'Yeah, I don't want it—you have it.' He was super freaked out and still shaking when he walked away. Then, someone else walked up to me and I was trying to tell them this story to build their faith. I said, 'He gave me the feather—it's right here.' I flipped through my Bible and there it was—right in Ezekiel 37, right in the passage about the Valley of Dry Bones. The man randomly put it in my Bible, but the Spirit of the Lord broke any doubt I had at that moment, saying to me, 'He was there, you know.'

For a number of years, the feather stayed in its place at Ezekiel 37—I always kept it there. Fast forward a few years, my wife Ruth and I were in the Philippines ministering with friends at Hosea Church. It was a wild night. At the end of the meeting, we were praying for people. Chairs were flying as people were falling out in the spirit, and people were pushing all the chairs and everyone's belongings out of the way to the sides of the church. It was a mess. At the very end of the service I was looking for my belongings and I said, 'Where's my Bible?' I found it, and then all of a sudden I thought, 'the feather!' I started thumbing through the pages and could not find it. It wasn't in Ezekiel 37, and I couldn't find it anywhere I looked. Everything was such a mess that Ruth never even found her Bible.

Over the next few days I looked through my Bible, thumbing through the pages, holding it upside down and shaking it. Heartsick, I literally turned every page looking for the feather and I was like, 'Lord, where's my feather?' It was to the point that when we had to leave the Philippines, I didn't want to leave without it. For three months, I didn't have it. Finally, I said to the Lord, 'Father, I want my feather back. We were praying for your people—I want that back.' Three months later I was sitting in our intercession group praying with our intercessors. All of a sudden I look down at my Bible and I see this white strand sticking out of it, and all I could say was, 'Oh, you're back!'

The Lord had put it into Ecclesiastes 7 this time. The subtitle for that chapter was "Wisdom for Life." The Lord just sovereignly did that in response to my prayers. After three months, the Lord brought it back to me and put it in my Bible.

We actually had this one professionally examined, and at first we didn't know who to take it to, so we took it to a couple of veterinarians who said it wasn't fowl, and it wasn't synthetic. You can always tell the difference with these kinds of feathers—they're more iridescent. The only thing that I can ever find in scripture as a reference to feathers and the angelic are cherubim and seraphim. They are the only ones I can reference that have feathers. My parishioner literally handed me a cherubim or seraphim's feather from an angel that was hovering over the Valley of Dry Bones bringing it life.

I actually have one more story about this feather. The Bible says in Mark 16:20 that God confirms the word preached with signs accompanying it. When we start talking about the Holy Spirit and about glory stories, He shows up with demonstrations and displays his power.

We have friends, Bill and Connie Wilson, who live in both Israel and Washington DC. Bill's favorite story is this feather story. Anytime he has anyone over and I'm there, he makes me tell this story. This one morning we're sitting at breakfast with some other guests and Bill says 'John, you have to tell them the feather story.' So I am sitting at a table with half a dozen other people and I tell them the same story that I just shared. The story ends and everyone breaks away and is taking their dishes to the kitchen, but hanging onto the last words. No one else is at the table, and it got quiet. I hear this "tink" sound and I look down in front of me and there's this diamond. I roll it around trying to see if it might be costume jewelry or it fell from someone's ring or something. Ruth even checked to make sure my diamond hadn't fallen out of my ring. All of a sudden, right before our eyes, the gem doubles in size. I put it in a Ziploc bag and brought it home until about 8 months later when another friend went back to Jerusalem and I handed her the bag and said, 'I want you to take this with you and bury it somewhere the Lord tells you to bury it for signs, wonders, and miracles in Israel.' She did that, and the stone is buried somewhere in Israel to this day.

John Filler, Pastor of Gateway Church, Coeur D'Alene

****

There is something spectacular about knowing that feathers can and literally do appear from another dimension—the heavenlies—and that we humans here on earth are not limited to what we can touch, feel, and see in this physical realm alone. God is able to help us even to the point of crossing dimensional barriers as was shown in this story. It brings the concept of "on earth as it is in heaven" (Matthew 6:10) to an entirely new level!

I would like to pray for each reader to receive this manifestation that God has shown my family and many others by His great grace:

Father, I ask that You grace each person who reads this today with the manifestation of feathers from heaven, with supernatural oil, manna, and everything else You have for him or her. I ask that You give us all new opportunities to learn and grow in this reality and to understand more and more about who You are in us. I ask that You pour out Your blessings upon us in a tangible manner so that we, too, can experience feathers from heaven as a demonstration of Your love and kindness. We thank You for Your goodness and grace, and we receive this gift freely because of Your great love for us in Jesus' name. Amen.

Works Cited

Chatwin, Bruce. *The Songlines*. London: Pan Books, 1988.

"Deceive". Dictionary.com Unabridged. Random House, Inc. 4
    Aug. 2016. <Dictionary.com
    http://www.dictionary.com/browse/deceive>.

Filler, John. Personal interview. 6 Mar. 2016.

Johnson, Tyler. *How to Raise The Dead*. Charleston, SC:
Createspace, 2010.

King, Michael. *Gemstones From Heaven*. USA: The Kings of Eden
Press, 2015. Kindle file.

Mulinde, John. "How Satan Steals Our Prayers: Combat in the
    Heavenly Realms." www.divinerevelations.info, Nov.
    2000. MP3

Strong, James. *Strong's Exhaustive Concordance*. Peabody, MA:
    Hendrickson, 2007. Blueletterbible.com. Web. 6 Apr.
    2016.

---. "Enowsh." *Strong's Exhaustive Concordance*. Peabody, MA:
    Hendrickson, 2007. Blueletterbible.com. Web. 6 Apr.
    2016.

---. "Iysh." *Strong's Exhaustive Concordance*. Peabody, MA:
    Hendrickson, 2007. Blueletterbible.com. Web. 6 Apr.
    2016.

---. "Malak." *Strong's Exhaustive Concordance*. Peabody, MA:
    Hendrickson, 2007. Blueletterbible.com. Web. 6 Apr.
    2016.

Tanner, Rev. Kenneth. "The God Who Sings Creation." The
Huffington Post. TheHuffingtonPost.com, 13 Feb. 2014. Web.
18 May 2016.

THANK YOU FOR PURCHASING THIS BOOK

Thank you for reading *Feathers From Heaven*. This book is the second in a series of books planned to help bring a deeper level of maturity, revelation, and experience to the body about these signs God is manifesting in the earth. The titles of the books in the God Signs series will be as follows:

Gemstones from Heaven

Feathers from Heaven

Gold Dust from Heaven

Oil from Heaven

Manna from Heaven

If you enjoyed this book, you can find more free content at www.thekingsofeden.com. Please consider leaving a review on Amazon.com so others can find this book more easily. Feedback is also welcomed by the author at thekingsofeden@gmail.com, and miracle stories such as ones found in this book are always welcome.

Other titles by Michael King include:

The Gamer's Guide to the Kingdom of God

Excerpt from

Gemstones From Heaven

Chapter 1

Our Personal Testimony

In January of 2015 (earlier this year) God told me that gemstones would begin to appear more frequently around us. I was excited, as I have seen this manifestation hundreds of times before in the past few years. More recently gems appeared very infrequently, and for a few reasons. Before going further, however, some of you readers may not have heard of this before, so let me explain.

In the early spring of 2012 a friend of mine, Carla, came for a visit. She is a musician and sound therapist; when she passes through Portland every so often, we and some other friends make sure to visit her. This particular visit she had a surprise for all of us, but we didn't know the half of it.

We went to a retired chiropractor's house to meet some other friends of hers who had come for a visit. All together there were nine of us present at this gathering. One couple had a unique manifestation of the Lord happen around them, something that had been going on for five years at that time— namely that gemstones from heaven would literally appear around them, both on the ground and in the air.

The stones themselves all have brilliant facets. Some of the facets are cut so strangely that it flabbergasts jewelers because people simply do not make jewelry this way. For example, I have a gem that is an irregular, rhomboidal shape. Out of the thousands I have seen appear, I have only once seen a raw, rough, uncut stone. The majority are amethysts, peridot, emerald, garnets, and rubies, along with an occasional aquamarine. There are also clear and yellow stones, probably different colors of topaz.

In all honesty, I cannot tell for certain what any of these stones are since I've never had any professionally tested, but some are pretty obvious just by looking at them. Since this started, I bought a diamond-tester. Very few of the ones I have found are diamonds, suggesting the clear and yellow ones are topaz or some other stone. Most of the gemstones are the size of the head of an eraser, and the teeny tiny ones are actually as uncommon as really large ones.

Each stone is unique, but some stand out more than others. On rare occasion there will be a mystic fire topaz, a stone that has three colors in it that are all mixed together. They are some of my favorites. Carnelian, an orange stone, rarely appear as well, and are a unique change when they do. My stepdaughter found a stone once that had streaks of gold in it, and she also found a raw stone once—the only uncut stone I have ever seen appear. Occasionally a larger jewel will show up including ones that are the size of a fingernail or larger. Rarer still, probably close to one in five-thousand gems or more, will be a stone that appears in a setting of some kind. This can be in a ring, cuff links, pendant, or earrings. On at least one occasion that I know of, the chain even appeared with the pendant!! In addition to all of these stones, from time to time a feather, usually at least an inch or two long, would appear in midair near one man. It was almost as if he was fluffing wings and stray feathers were falling off.

Sometimes the gems will grow in size; they can be prayed for when chipped and heal, even multiply! One of our grandchildren put one in a box once, and when she opened the box again, a second smaller one that was otherwise identical was sitting next to it. The gem had a baby!

Sunshine, my wife, and I were like little children that first evening, running around and picking up gemstones off of the floor. Sometimes we would hear them fall out of midair and land on the hardwood floors, sounding like a muted version of a rain stick—the wooden musical devices filled with beans or seeds to make rattling noises.

Other times we simply found them on the surfaces where they appeared, such as on a coffee table or windowsill. At one point we laid down on the floor in the middle of the foyer and I asked God to hit us with gems. I remember having my eyes closed and feeling something hit my shoulder then heard the sound of rattling across the floor. We both shouted with great delight, and I can still remember my wife's excitement as she went around picking them up. She is so child-like when they fall. To this day she still squeals with joy every time she finds one, and I have to imagine God loves that.

That first weekend my wife and I experienced this manifestation was a whirlwind. We spent that Friday night in an evening of worship, fellowship, laughter, and gemstone-hunting throughout the house. Carla is a pianist and led us in some worship songs on the Baby Grand piano in the chiropractor's living room. We took communion in an "upper room," i.e. one of the upstairs bedrooms, and as a whole, God just rocked our night.

Saturday was a bit of a mental break, as our minds attempted to process the absolutely amazing experiences we had the night before. Although "break" is sort of a relative term. I must have called at least four friends and told them all about our experience and what God had been doing.

Sunday was a blast. We went to church and shared with a bunch of people what we had experienced. That evening we went to another meeting that ministry couple held at a church on the other side of the city. That night was really fun too, because not only did we have our new friends there, but a pair of our long-time friends, Hope and Beth, drove several hours to reach the gathering. Hope and Beth are precious women and are both what I refer to as God-junkies—they will go anywhere and do almost anything if God is in it. When we told them about the gems, their response was, "Where do we need to be and when?"

We spent Sunday evening listening to the husband, whom the manifestation seemed to center around, share about his life journey and how God brought him salvation as well as this unique gem miracle years later. The people at that church were very kind, and so many people wanted to share the gems to make sure everyone had at least one. It was like a room full of starving people, but each one made sure the other had a piece of bread before they were content to eat their own. This meeting showed me how hungry people are to see God work miraculously in their lives. We *all* desire a visible demonstration of the invisible God, and even more, a tangible demonstration of His love for us.

For myself, the mind-blowing experience just continued. I felt *so* incredibly loved by my Heavenly Father, who loved me so much that he would not only obliterate my experience of "impossible," but do it with such beautiful and valuable items. I mean, how many other gods have we ever heard of that hand out gemstones to their followers?

A year or so later, we invited the couple with the gems to hold a Gem Party at our house—a twelve-hour revolving door of fellowship, food, and fun. During the day we had a very informal hang-out, and people of all ages were literally crawling on our carpet picking up stones. In the evening we had a more focused time of worship and the man shared his testimony, similar to the one I heard a year prior.

At that time they brought out some of the more spectacular gemstones God has given them. Many of these are large, and by large I mean the size of a quarter or larger.

From talking to friends, counting my own bag of gems, and observing the gems others picked up, I estimated that over four-thousand gems appeared in that twelve hours.

I will be honest; I consider this a conservative estimate, based on the number of people present and the quantity of gems each of them left with, and I suspect the number approaches six-thousand. At the end of that meeting, I had over one-hundred gems myself; that didn't include the massive amount my wife, stepdaughter, her husband and my grandkids each had, or the stashes that the other twenty-six people who came left with by the end of the day. Some people left with far more than I did!

This meeting sparked something, and we held one every two to three months for the rest of that year. Not only that, but it turned into a series of meetings throughout the surrounding area. Gem Parties have been held at four or more different people's houses since then, the most recent one happened almost a year and a half after we stopped holding meetings at our house.

Fast forward again to January of this year, three years after we first experienced the gem manifestation and a year after we stopped having meetings, we still had gems show up but it was usually one gem with a four-month interval in-between. I prayed and talked to God about this and reminded Him that His Word says when we honor someone we can have their reward. I repented for any ways we had been dishonoring to the gem-ministers (as all relationships have conflicts and this was no different), and asked God to fix anything that was hindering the flow of gems in our lives. Shortly thereafter, God told me that gems would begin to appear again and with greater frequency. When he told me this I was excited, but also somewhat reserved. After all, a single stone every month would be more frequent than what we had experienced the previous year prior, and God has a way of doing things very differently than what we imagine it will look like.

To my amazement, on January 31, within a week and a half of God telling me the gems would increase, I found the first stone. It was a clear white color and conspicuously perched on the edge of my granddaughter's bed. She had fallen asleep in our bed and I was taking her downstairs at midnight to tuck her into her own. As I drew near to the bed and saw it, I immediately recognized the gem for what it was. I showed my wife, who, yet again, squealed with delight.

The next one appeared on my stepdaughter's wedding day on our back patio—a wedding gift from our Heavenly Father. On Saturday, May 23, we had a gem-breakout while we were replacing our dining room carpet with flooring. Since we were pulling up the carpet, I told everyone to be on the lookout for gems in case any had appeared *under* the carpet when we held the Gem Parties years before. Sure enough, my stepdaughter found one while I was out at Home Depot. Go figure.

Something in this process, whether our faith and expectation or something else entirely, sparked a supernatural whirlwind. For the rest of that weekend, into the next week and for weeks afterward, gems appeared. They started by simply showing up on the floor and on the window ledges, but after a few hours advanced to falling out of midair onto the new flooring. In fact, it became so prolific and distracting that it took us two days to complete what would have been a one-day project, but God wasn't done. To date, we had never seen a blue sapphire appear, and we had a handful of them appear that weekend!

While that may not seem significant to some, blue sapphires hold special significance to my wife and me in regards to our marriage. Blue sapphires are an older tradition than diamonds for marriage. Sunshine's nickname for her unknown "man-to-be" even before we ever met was Blue Sapphire. Once, before we were even seeing each other much less got married, she was wearing a blue sapphire ring and I prophesied over it. I also had a blue sapphire ring on my wedding finger in the spirit realm which God had given me years before we met. When blue sapphires began to appear it felt like God had taken this now-familiar manifestation to an even deeper place of love and meaning for us.

At the writing of this book we have not yet had any more gemstone-whirlwinds, but gems have continued to steadily appear around us, and I am encouraged that God is releasing this manifestation to the earth at a new level. Two years ago was the seventh-year anniversary for the gem manifestation starting, and we have now entered into the second seven-year cycle. It feels to me like we are part of a second-generation of this manifestation, where God is opening up new and exciting things and the circle of glory is spreading out even wider into the earth.